THE GREAT SOUTH BAY

A Picture Book

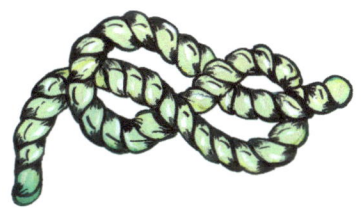

JEANINE O'GRADY

ISBN: 978-0-692-05922-7

Library of Congress Control Number:
2018901538

Book and cover design by Wordzworth
www.wordzworth.com

Published by South Shore Betty
www.southshorebettyny.com

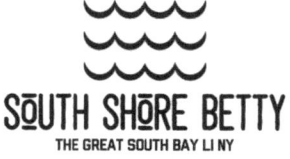

SOUTH SHORE BETTY
THE GREAT SOUTH BAY LI NY

For my husband T.J., my beautiful Saige Margaret and my sister Nicole

"A SMOOTH SEA NEVER MADE A SKILLED SAILOR"

FRANKLIN D. ROOSEVELT

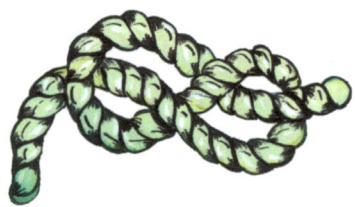

Introduction

The Great South Bay, actually a lagoon, is situated between Long Island and Fire Island, in the State of New York. It is approximately 45 miles long and protected from the Atlantic Ocean by Fire Island, as well as the eastern end of Jones Beach Island and Captree Island.

Long Island's South Shore, includes Lindenhurst, Town of Babylon, Town of Islip, Oakdale, Sayville, Bayport, Blue Point, Patchogue, Bellport, Shirley, and Mastic Beach. These towns are historic bay towns, with a rich history of clamming, fishing and boating.

The Great South Bay is home to the greatest fishermen. They can be spotted fishing off piers and on their boats. Our fishermen pick the most magnificent lures to catch the **biggest** fish on Long Island.

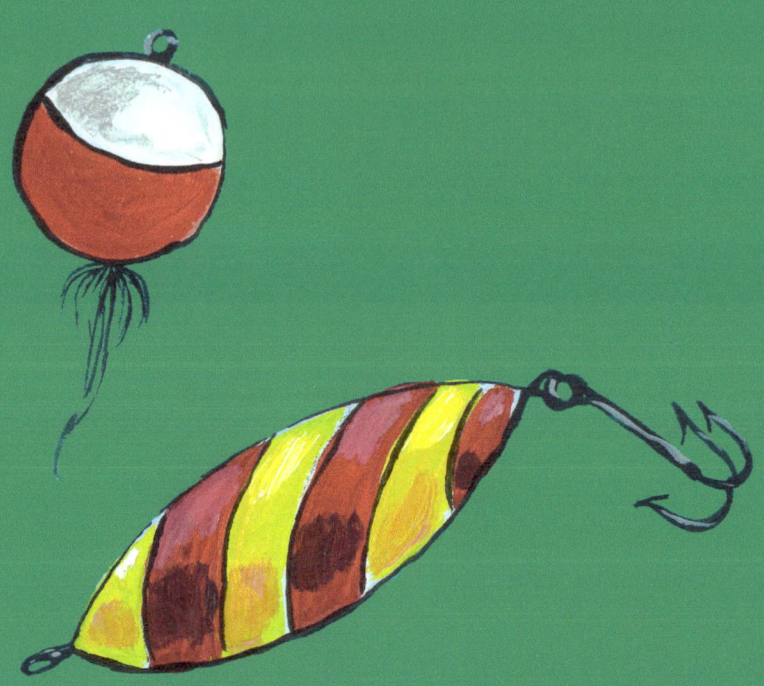

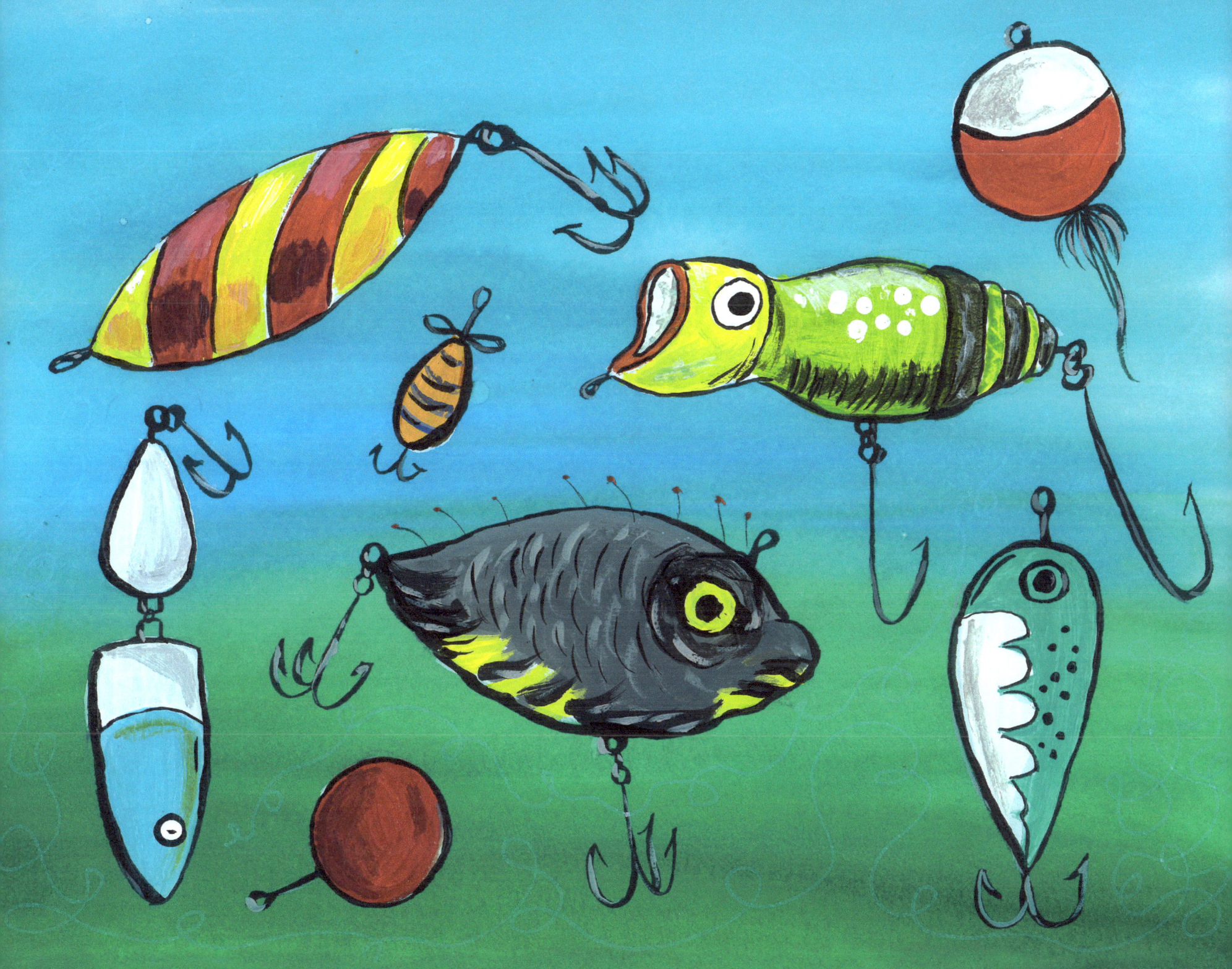

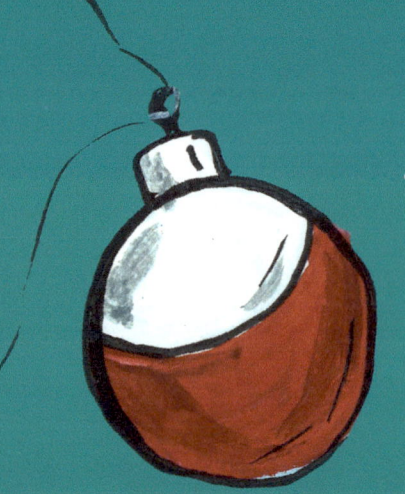

The Bluefish are a nice pastime for fishermen while waiting for the striped bass. The Bluefish flood through the bay in the Spring. The Bluefish stays deep and feed on bait fish.

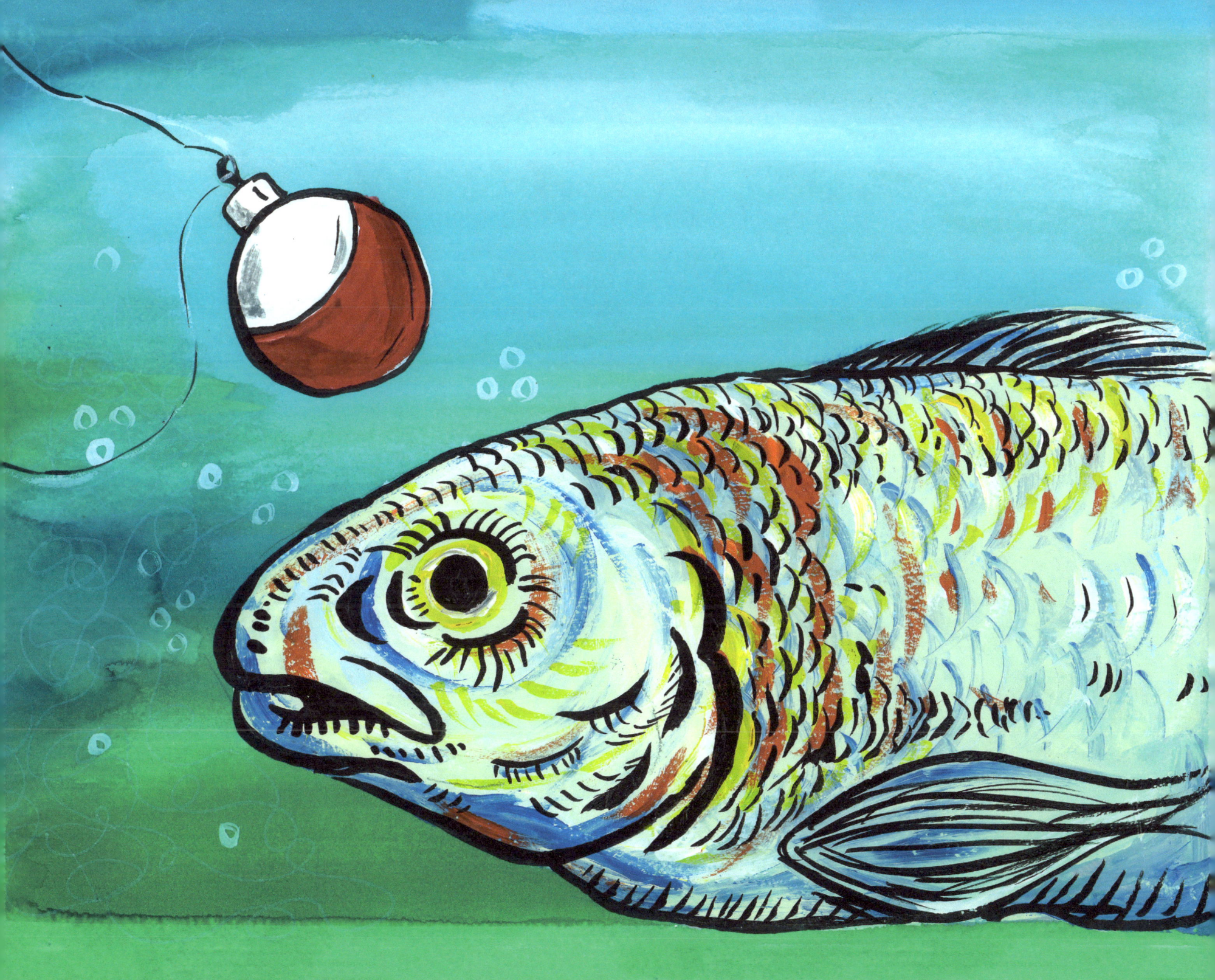

Fishing boats can be seen all around, buoy markers such as these bright red ones can help fishermen as a point of reference to locate their position.

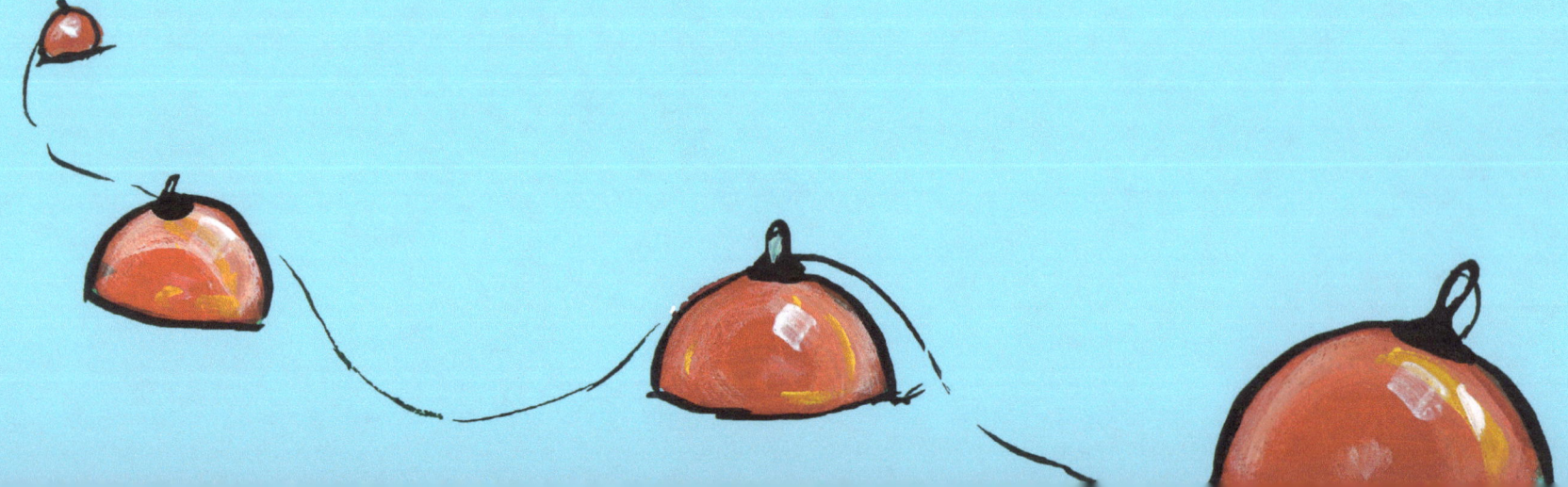

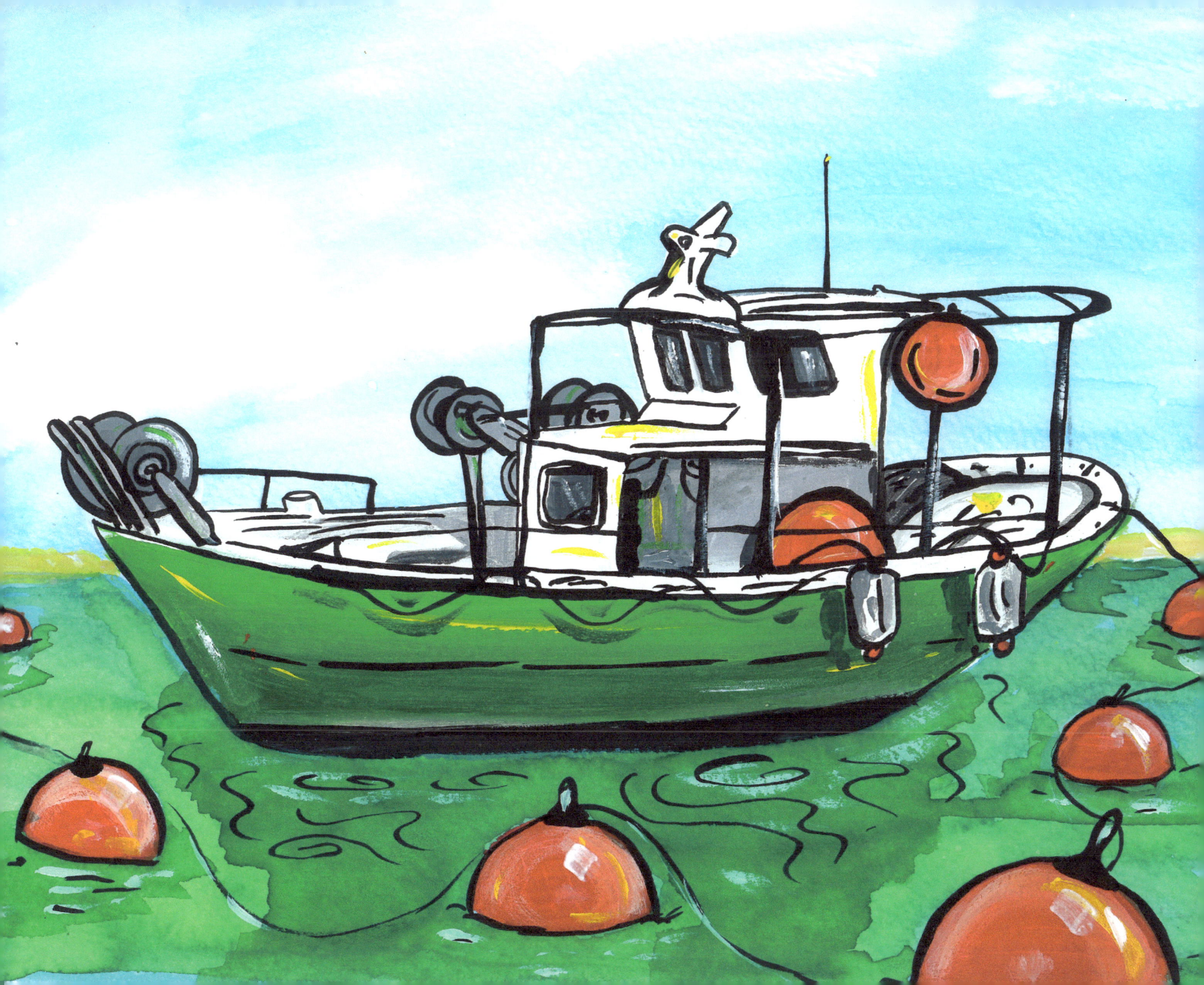

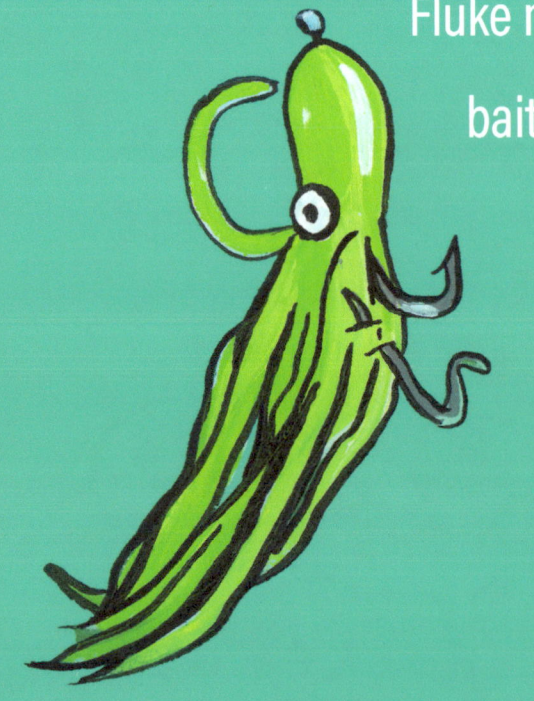

Fluke move into the bay during April, most fluke fishermen use baits such as spearing and squid.

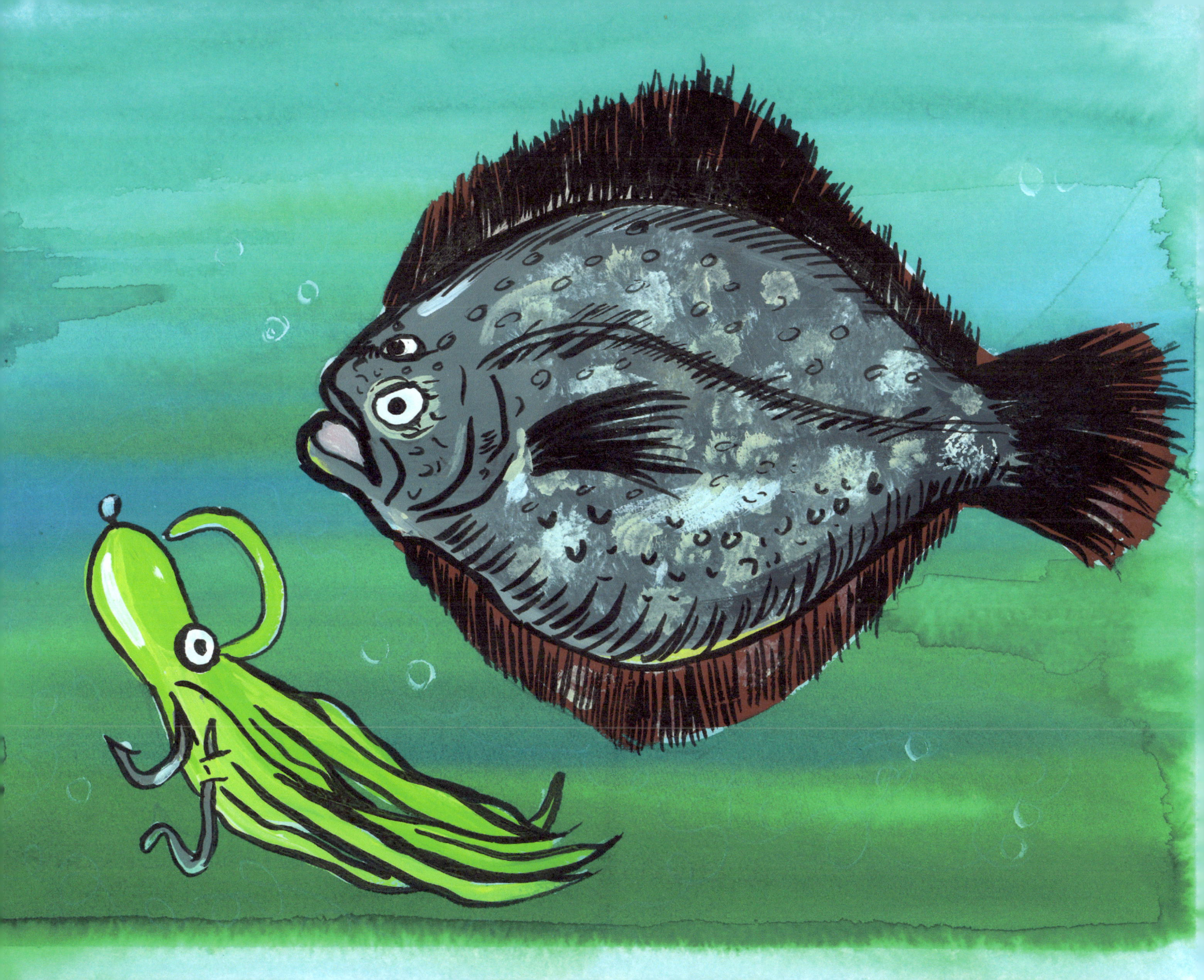

Clamming and crabbing boats can be spotted all along the bay. Once upon a time more than half the clams and Blue crabs eaten in the country came from the Great South Bay, they also filtered 40% of the water in the bay every single day, today they filter about 1% of this body of water. Without shellfish water quality declines and creatures that rely on clams, scallops and oysters as a food also suffer.

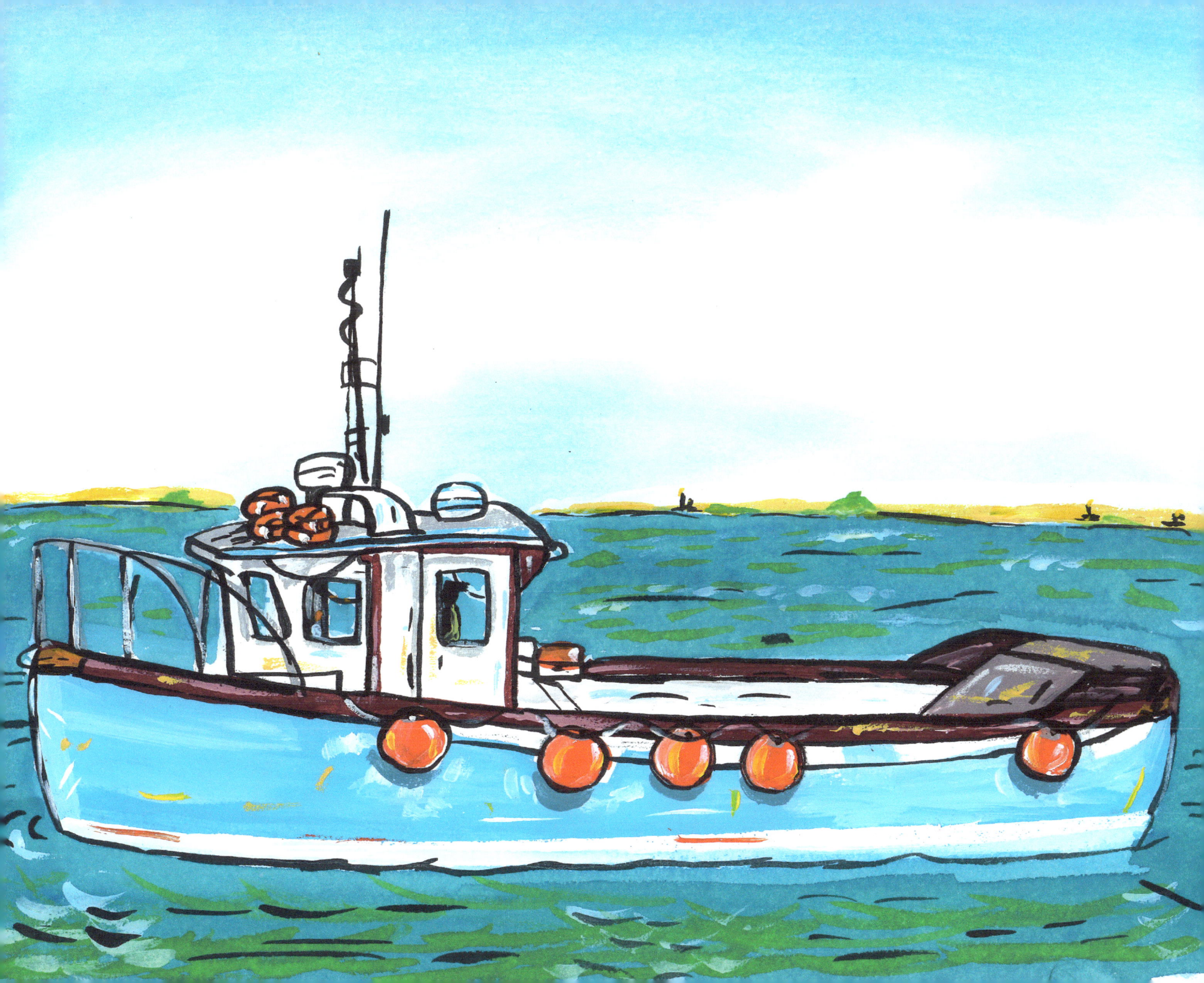

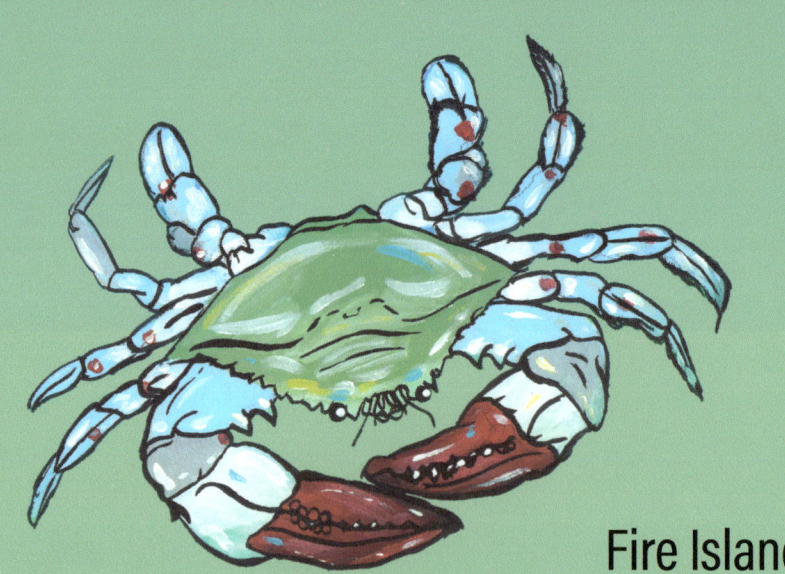

One of the most important shellfish in the waters surrounding the Great South Bay and Fire Island is the Blue Crab. Folks both young and old can be seen around crabbing off bridges, docks, and in the bay.

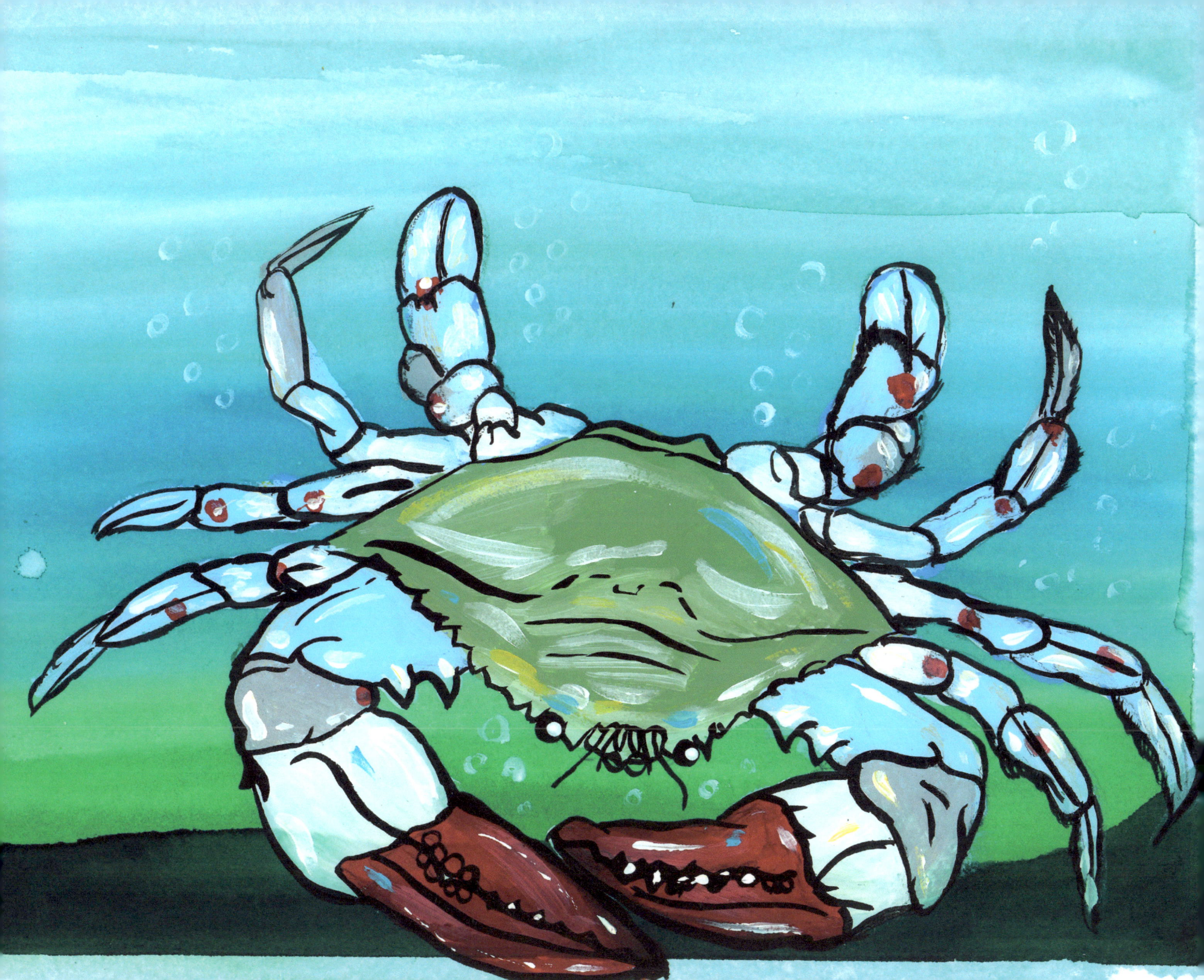

The Great South Bay is the original home of the "Blue Points", the Blue Point oyster is returning to the Great South Bay after almost completely disappearing from the world market place. Over-farming, pollution and hurricane Sandy had severely damaged the Blue Point oyster business. Now the population is growing in and around the bay due to new oyster farmers. We are very grateful for the efforts of these amazing individuals.

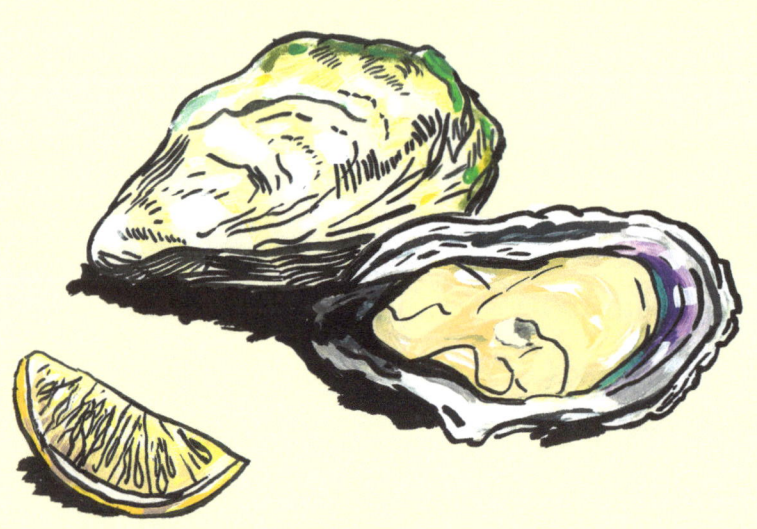

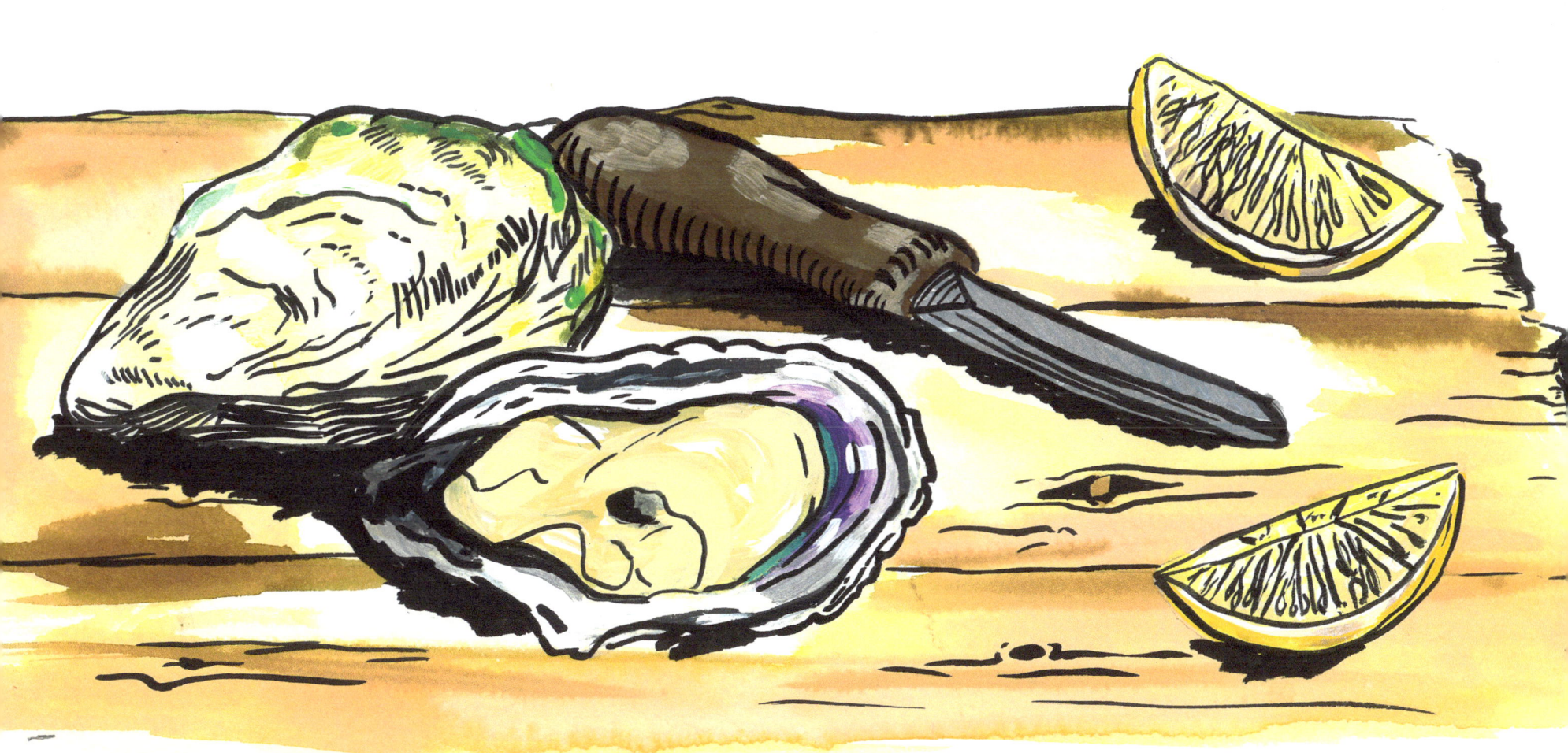

Our sea captains are top notch. They have the most swirly beards. Some sea captains have even reported seeing mermaids playing in the mist along the Fire Island sea shore.

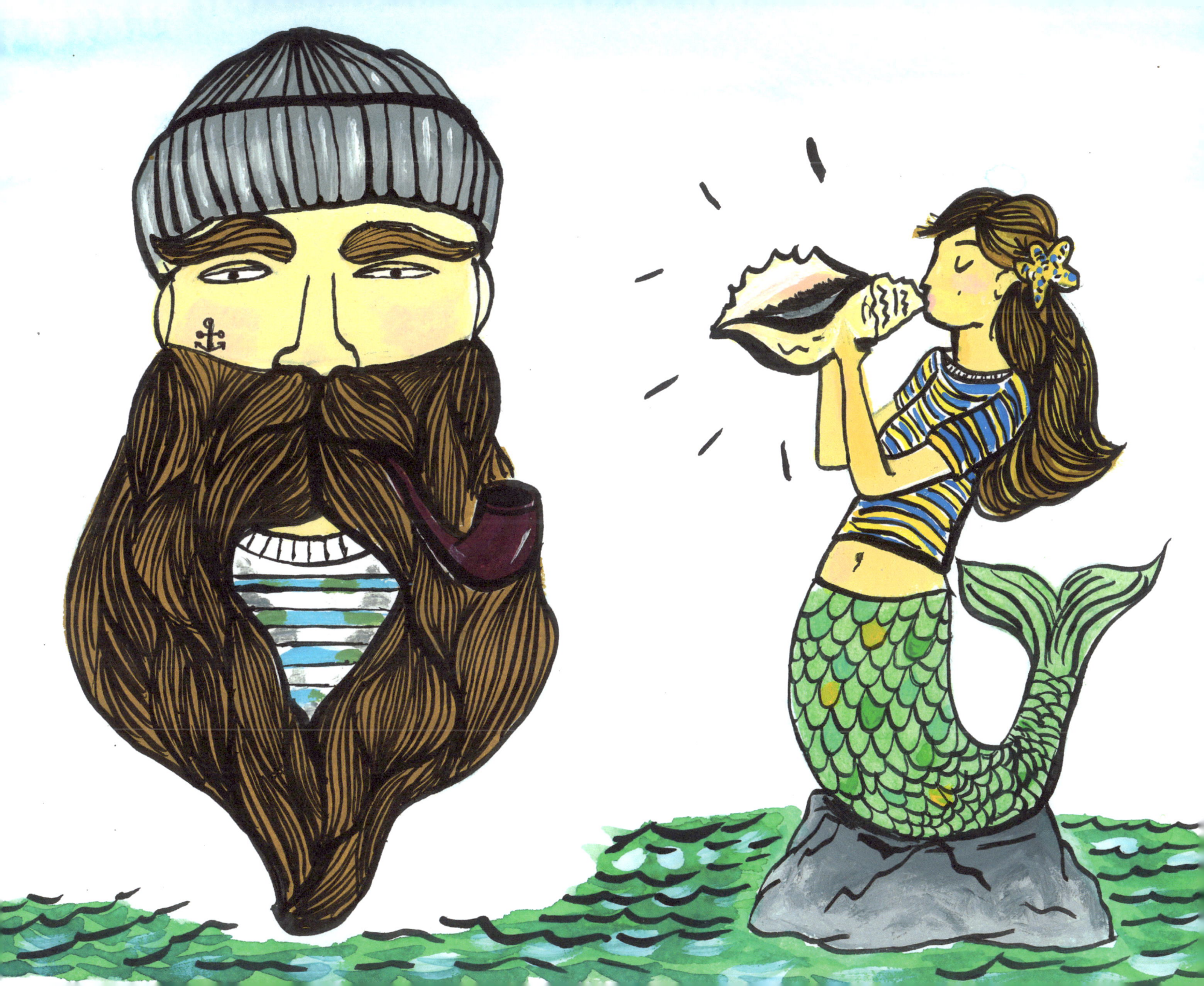

The Great South Bay and the South Shore of Long Island are home to the best fish markets in New York, these hardworking folks ensure we have the freshest catches around.

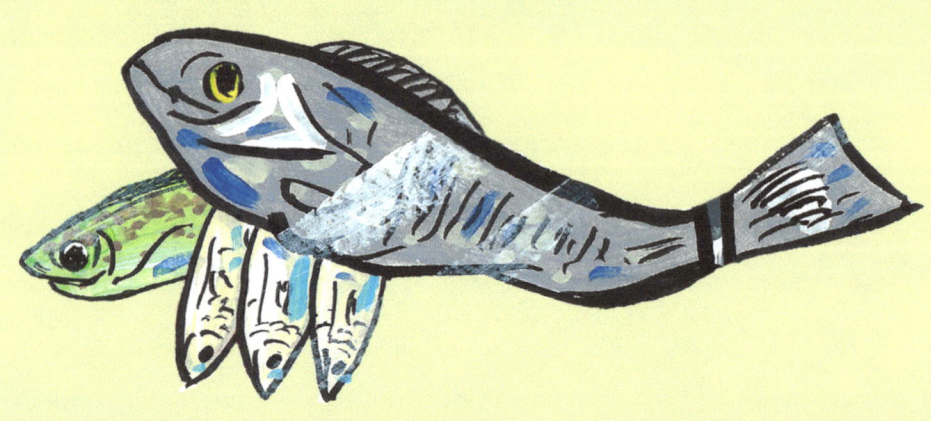

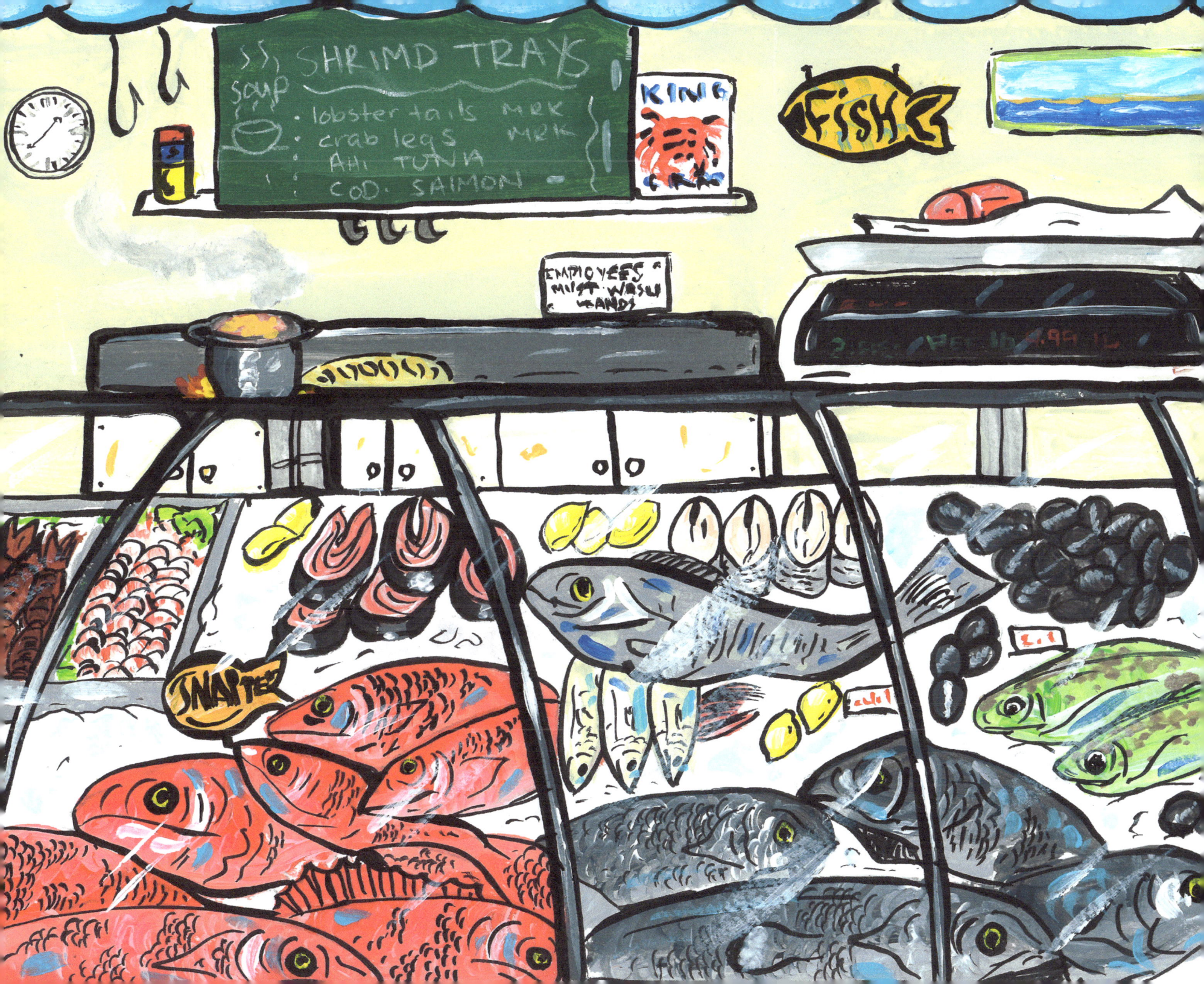

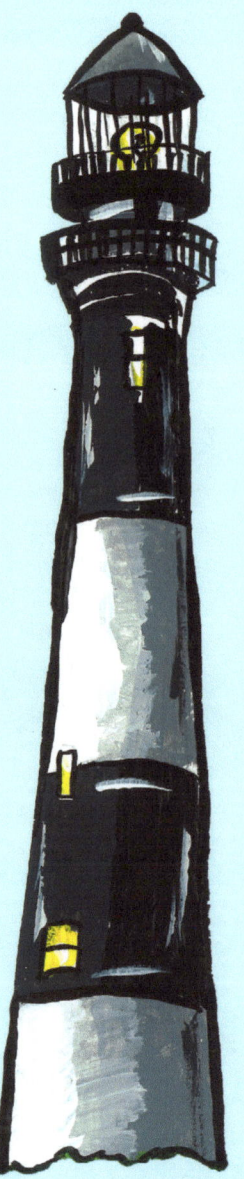

The Fire Island Lighthouse is a landmark on The Great South Bay it is located on the Western end of Fire Island. The Light house opened in 1858 and is 167′ tall, all that stands of the original is a circle of bricks.

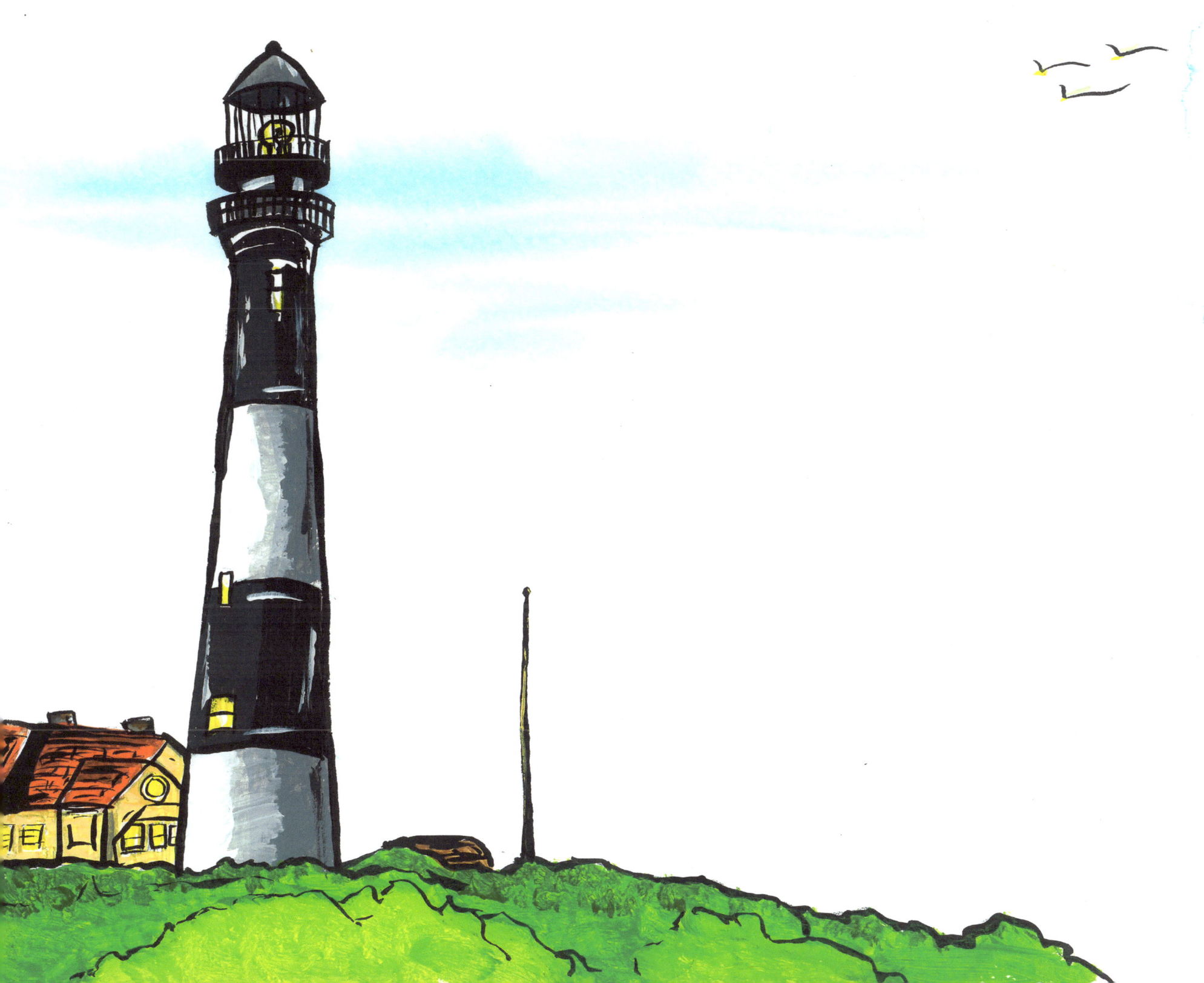

The Captree Bridge and The Great South Bay Bridge connect Robert Moses causeway from Long Island's mainland over The Great South Bay, connecting to both Captree and Jones Beach Island. There are many places to paddleboard and Gilgo beach is great for surfing.

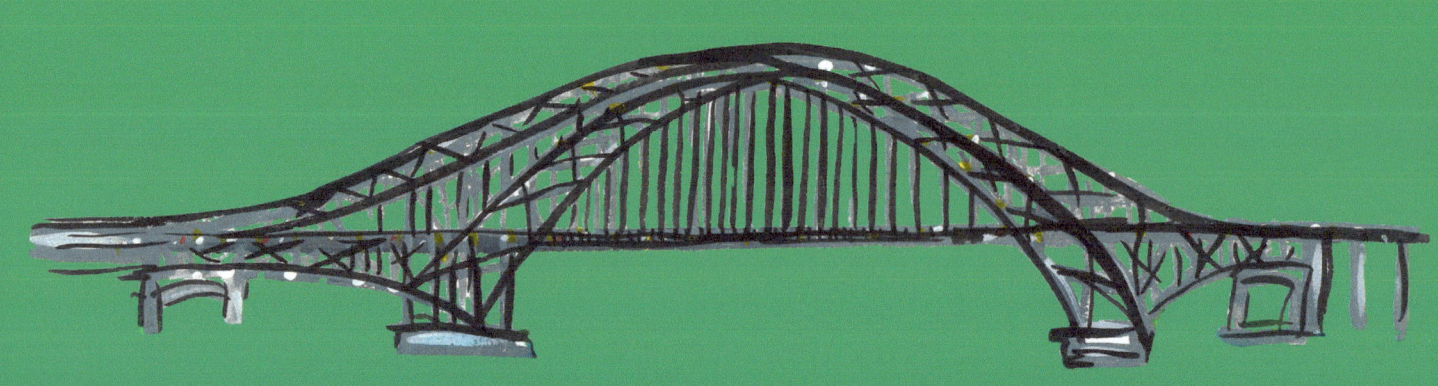

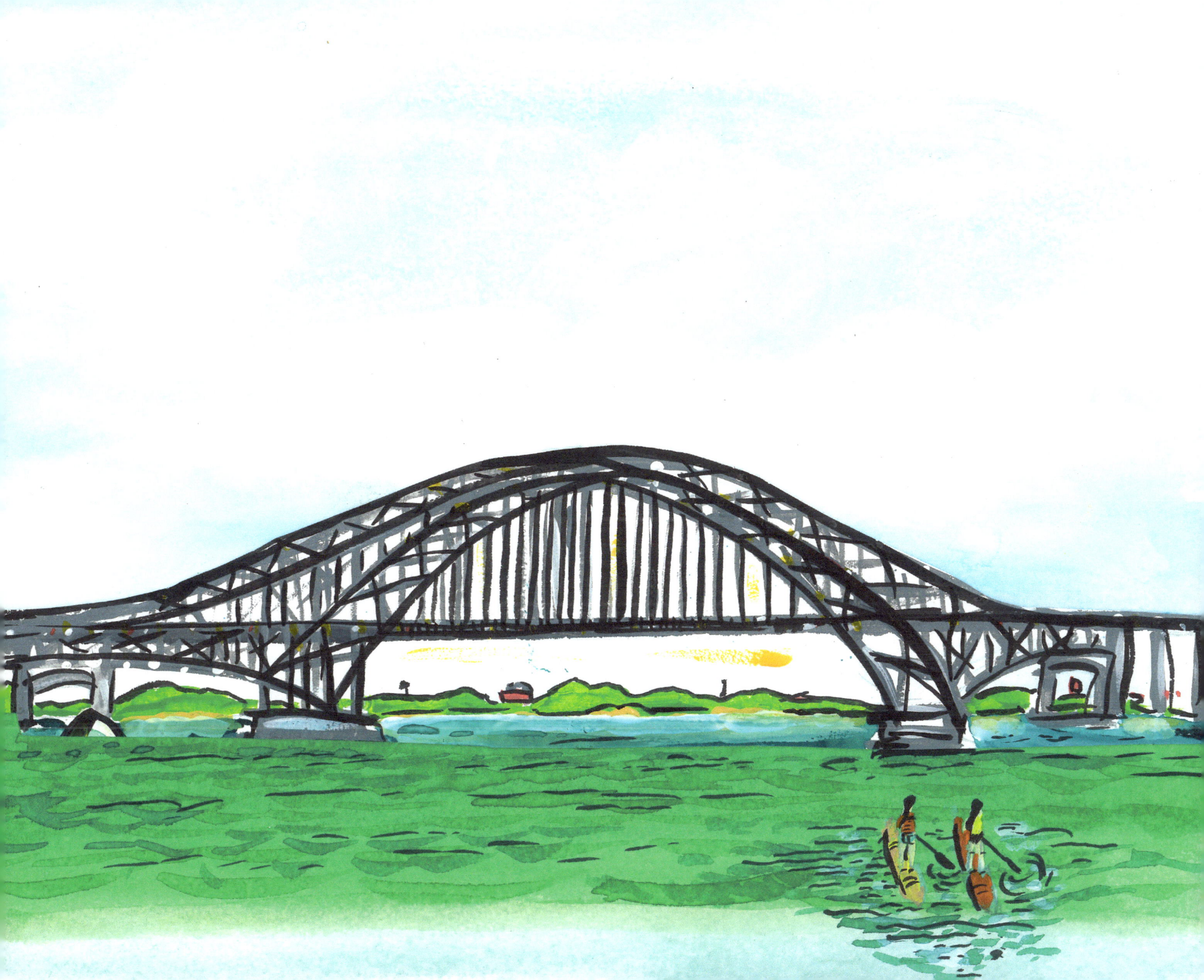

Sailing has been a Long Island pastime for centuries, surrounded by the Great South Bay, it is no wonder why this water sport is a favorite of both locals and visitors alike, not only is it fun to sail, but enjoying the beauty of sailboats is a joy that people on the shores simply can't pass up.

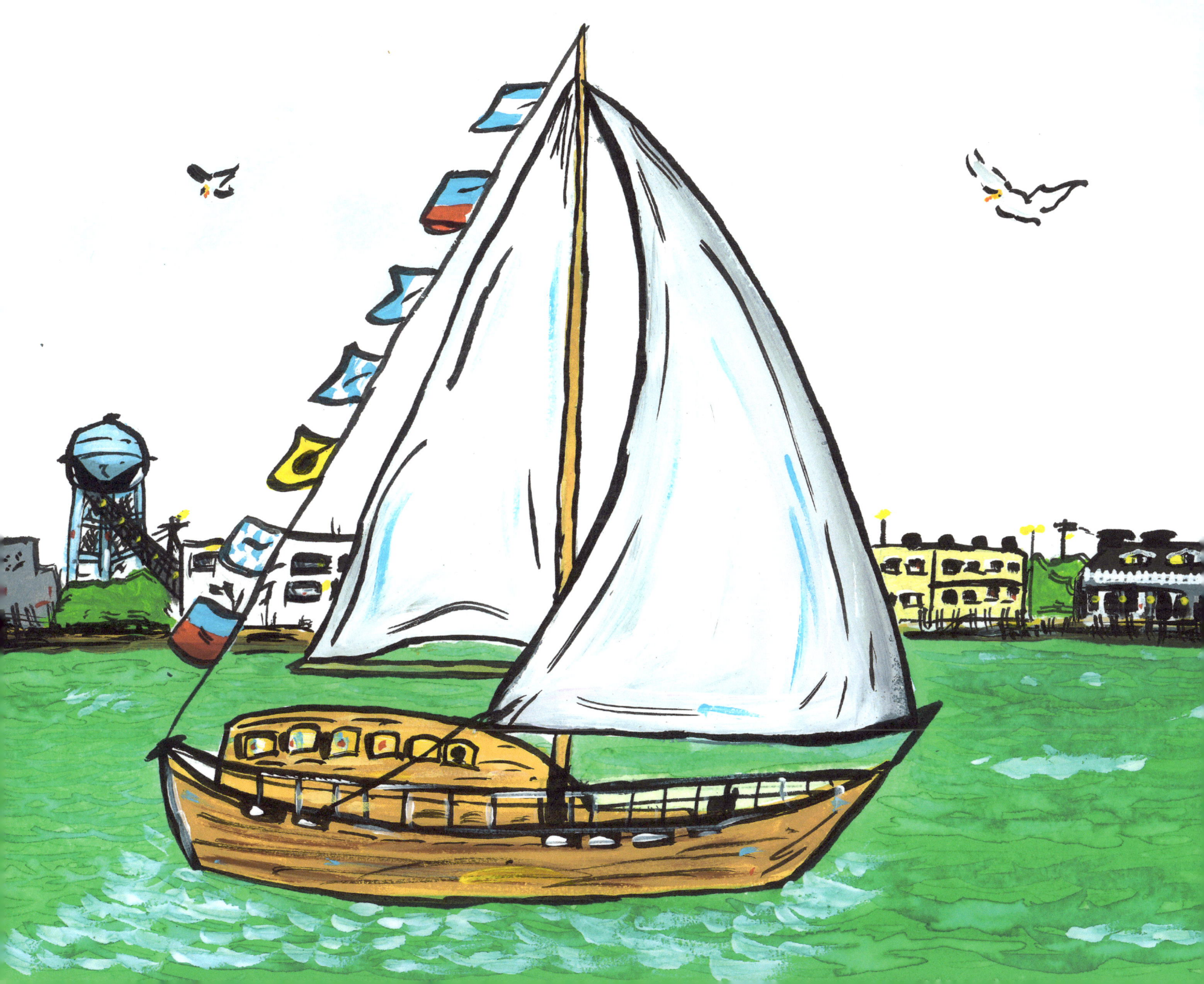

Every sailor needs knowledge of the variety of sailing knots and their different uses and drawbacks. Some knots include the figure of eight and the overhand.

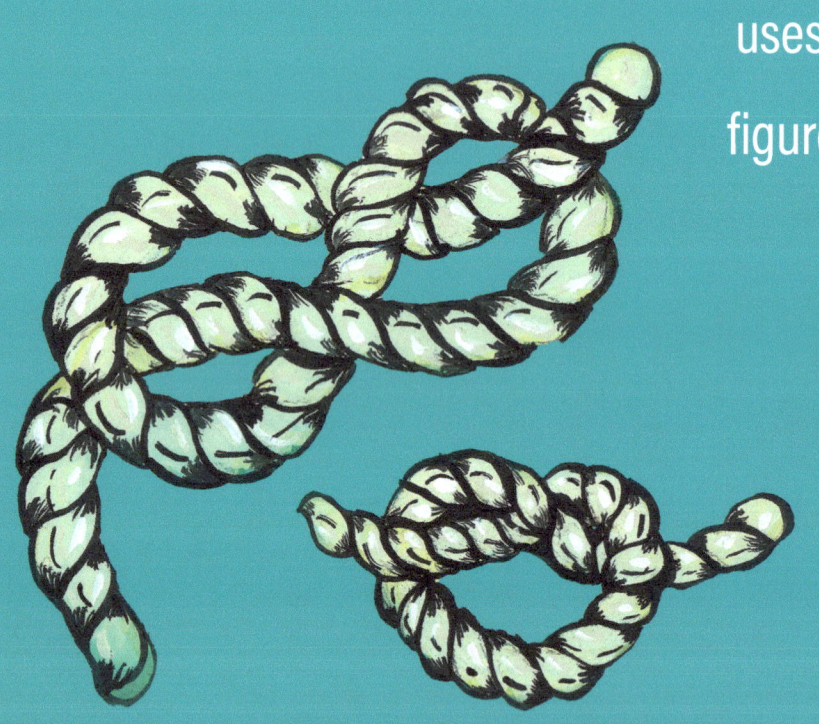

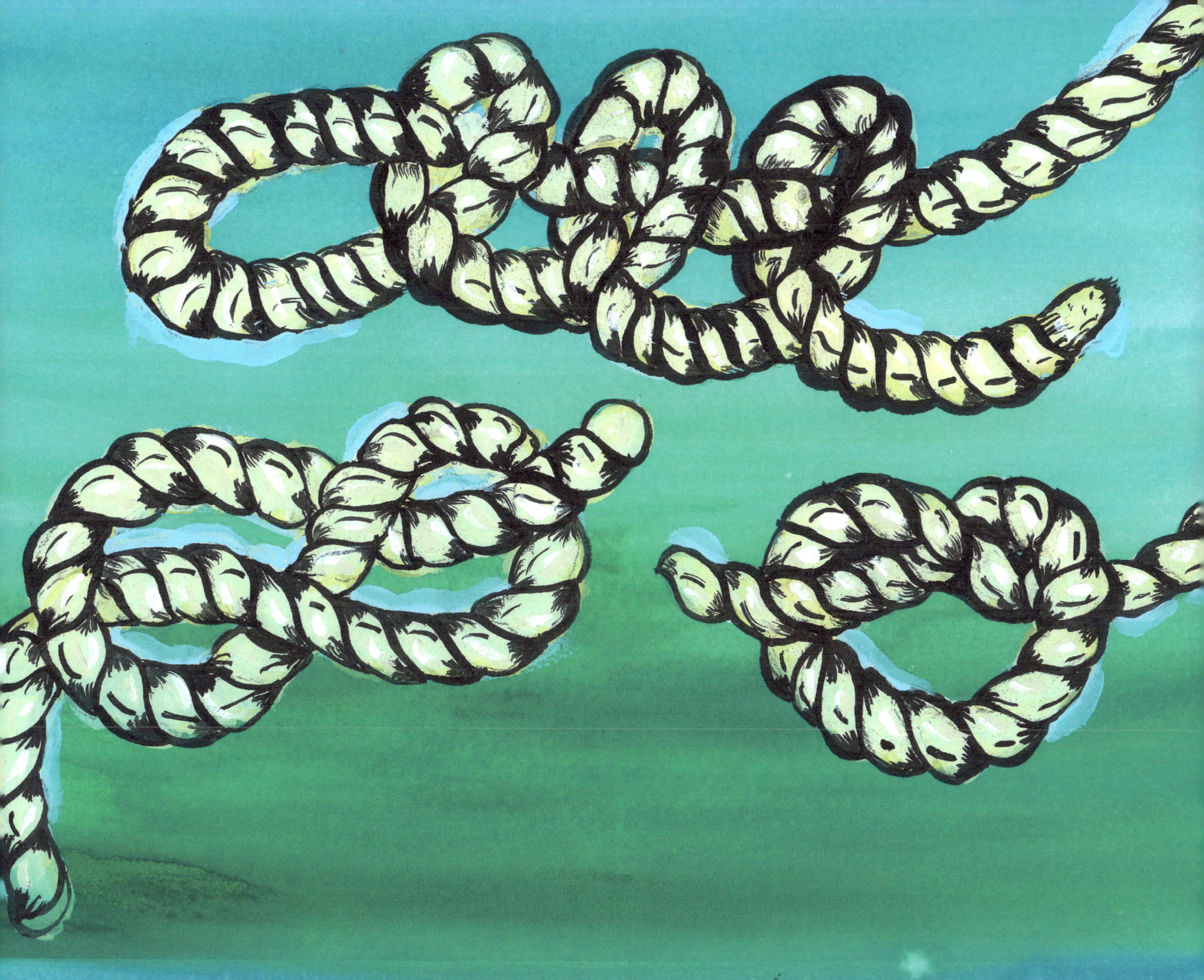

The ferries work non-stop to bring people back and forth from the mainland to Fire Island. The captain and crew work hard to ensure that everything runs smooth. The captains look out for buoys and markers, they are the "traffic signals" that guide the vessel operators safely along some water ways. The most famous is "Crazy Charlie" which rapidly sways back and forth.

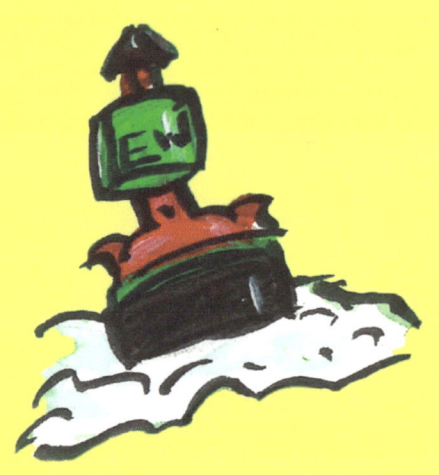

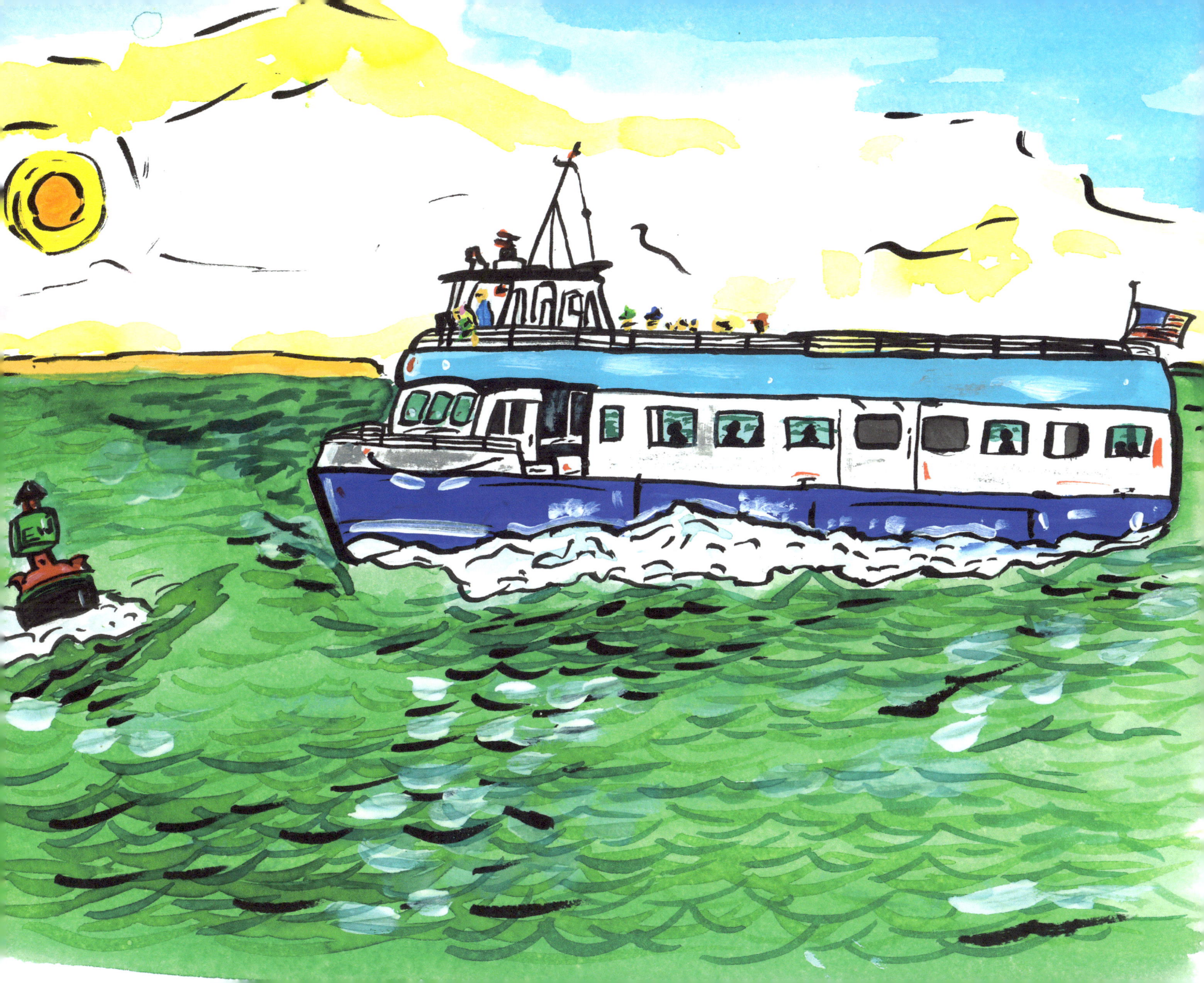

When staying on Fire Island do not forget your red wagon. The red wagon is a staple among families needing help bringing their vacation supplies back and forth. Children can also be seen selling hand PAINTED sea shells and lemonade out of the wagon.

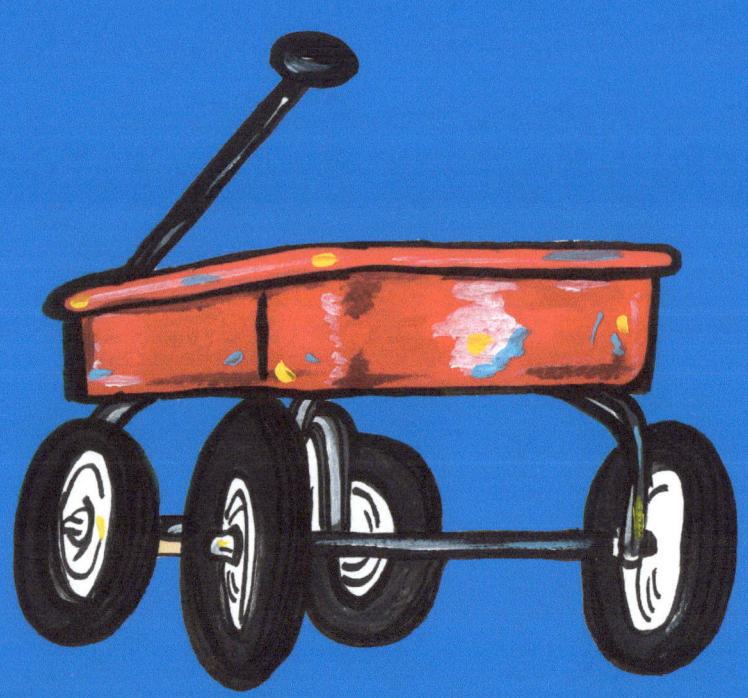

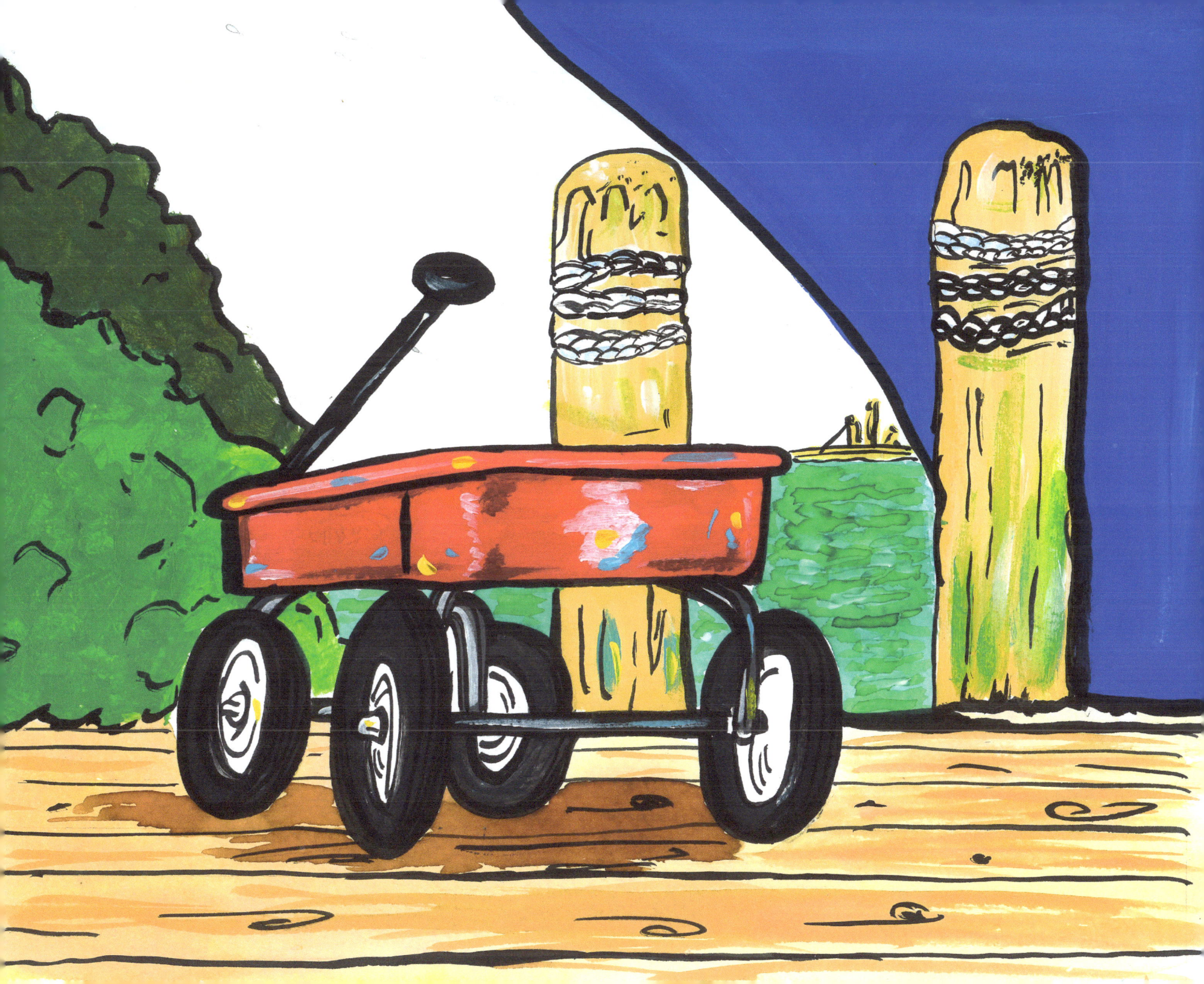

Our beaches on the South Shore are full of treasures. All you need is a keen eye. Some of the most beautiful sea glass can be found on our shores. Just bend down and wait till your eye catches one of these sparkling gems.

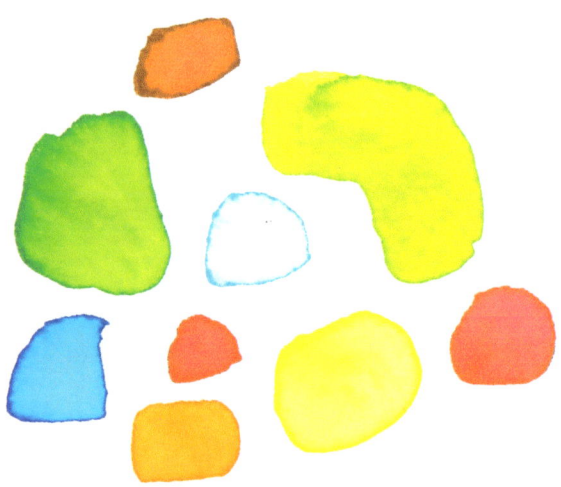

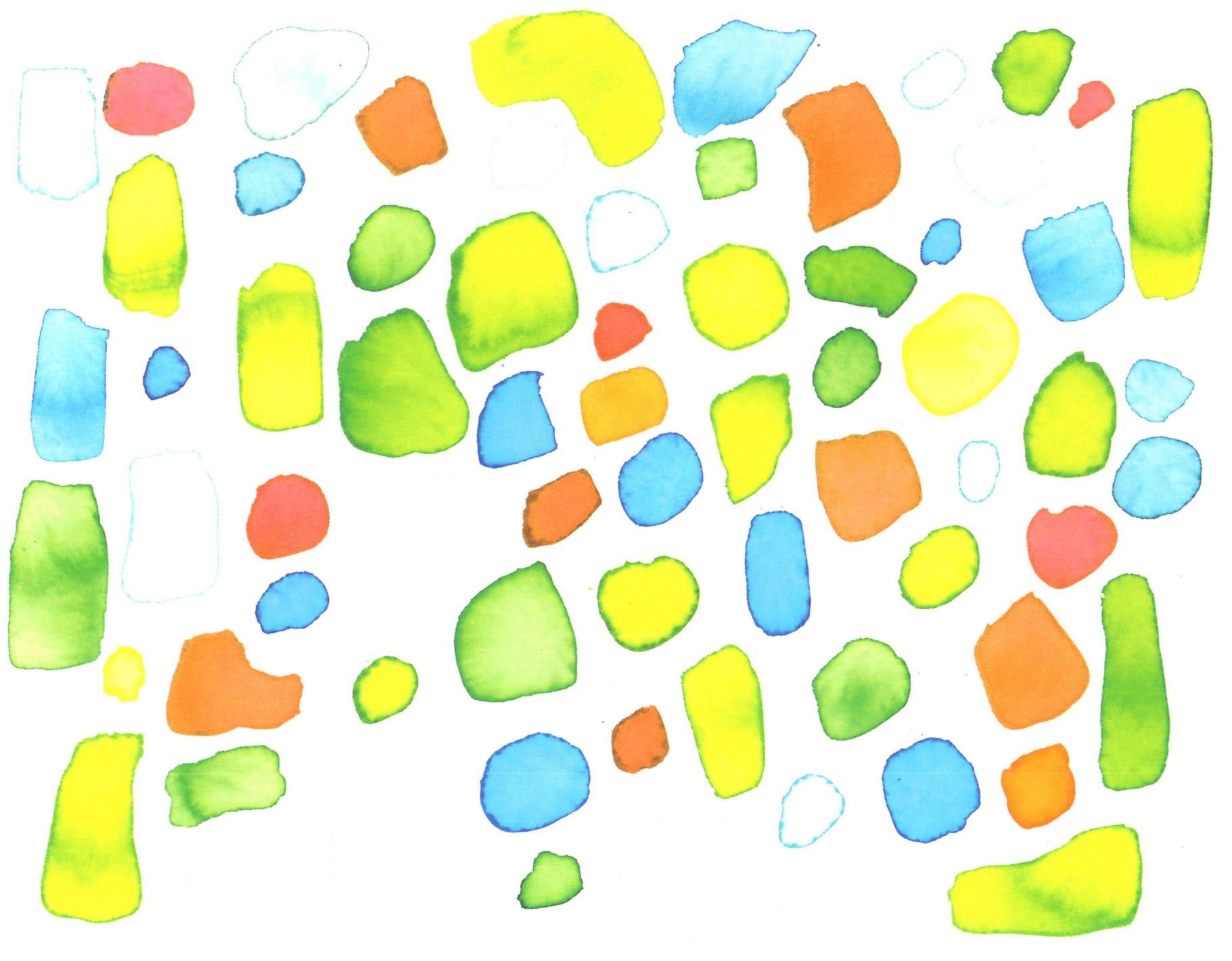

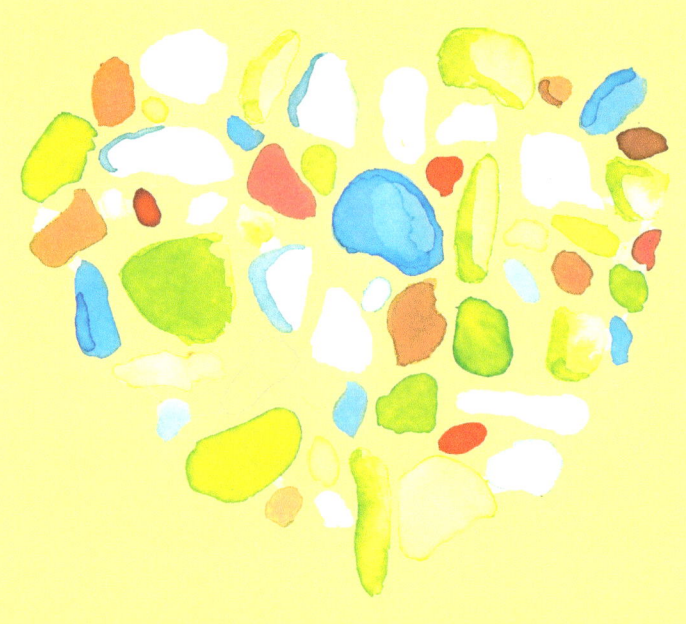

We love hunting for sea glass!

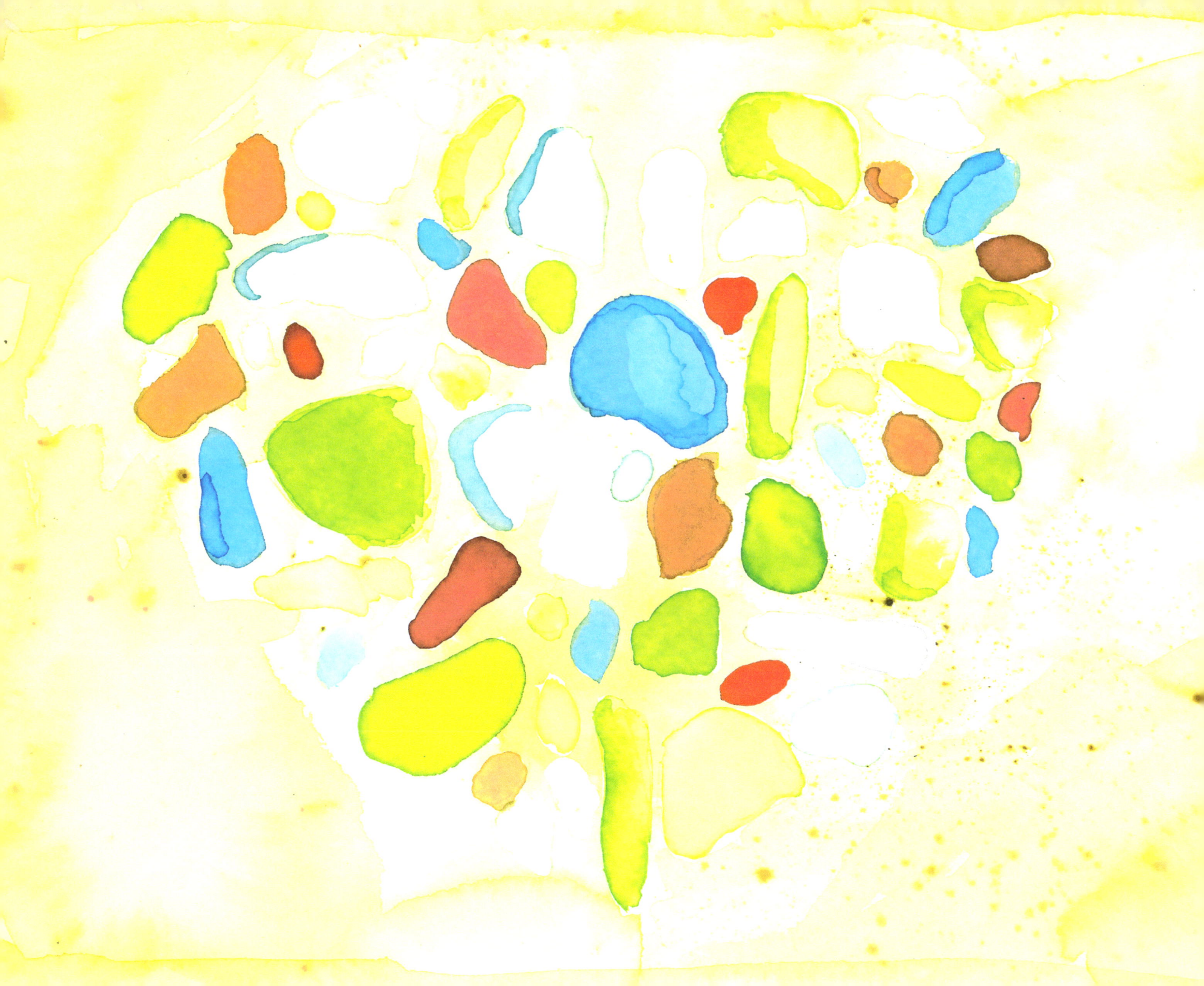

There are several wetlands located in and around The Great South Bay, local species include beautiful birds such as the Blue heron which can be seen standing in waters. The wetlands serve as a natural habitat for many species of plants and animals and absorb the forces of flood and tidal erosion to prevent loss of upland soil.

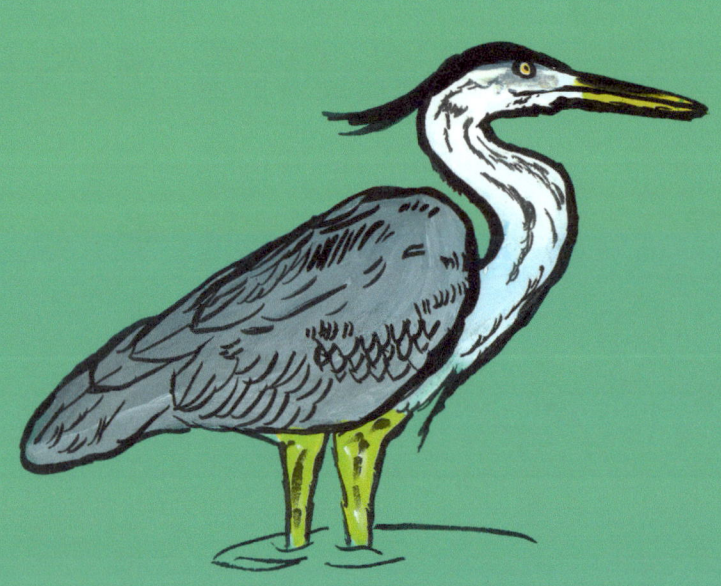

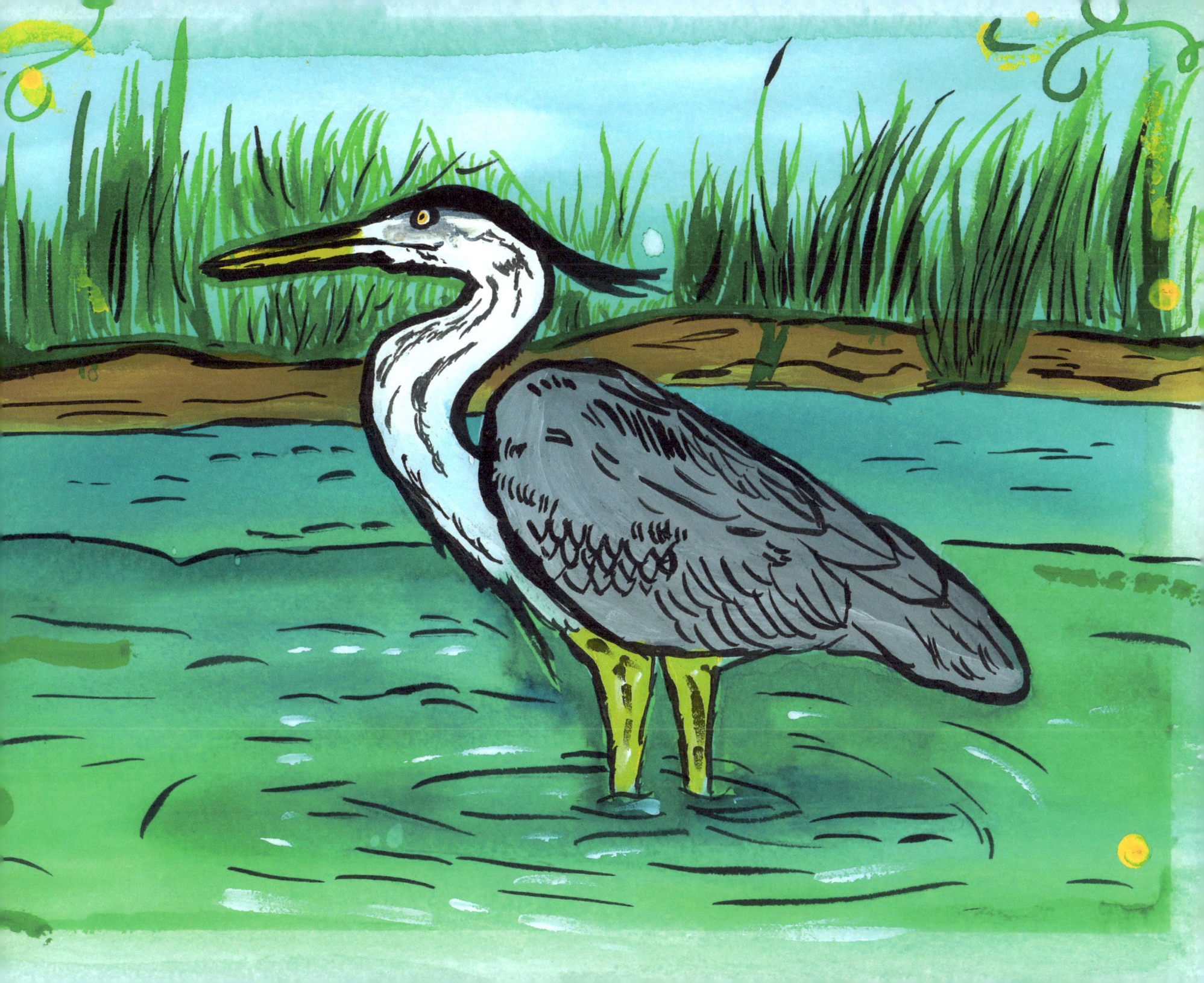

You can always hear the seagulls calling and the gentle roar of the crashing waves. Some locals consider the seagulls to be a nuisance species, they especially love to fly down and grab your French fries.

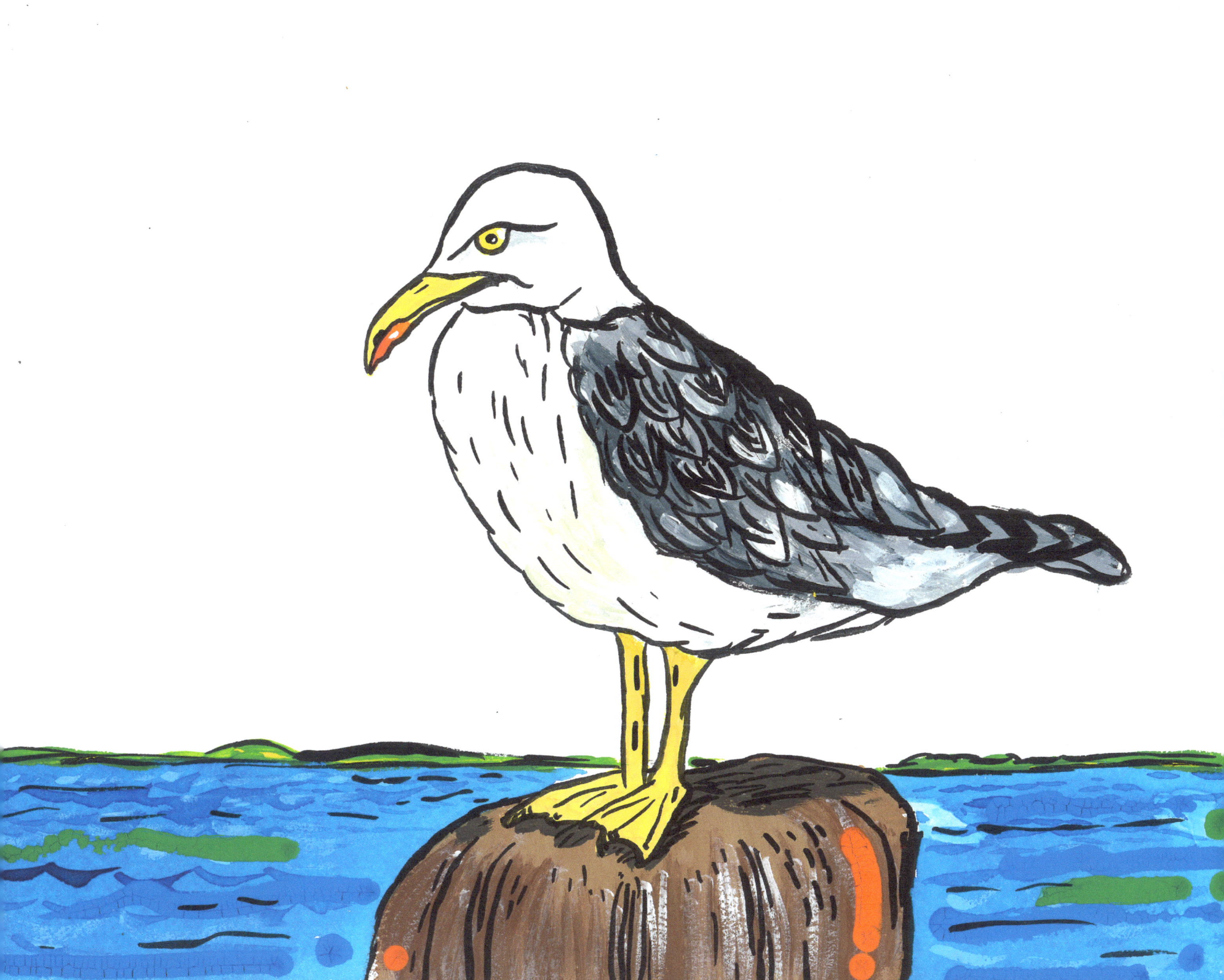

Sea Turtles such as the loggerhead and other marine creatures are home to The Great South Bay, they mistake plastic bags and other garbage for food such as jelly fish and eat it. It is important to be good stewards to our land and sea.

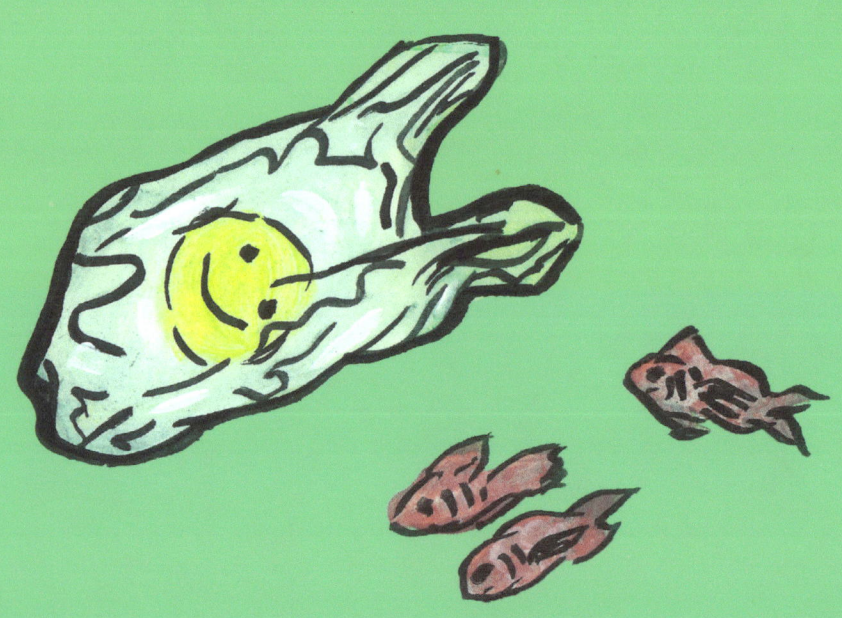

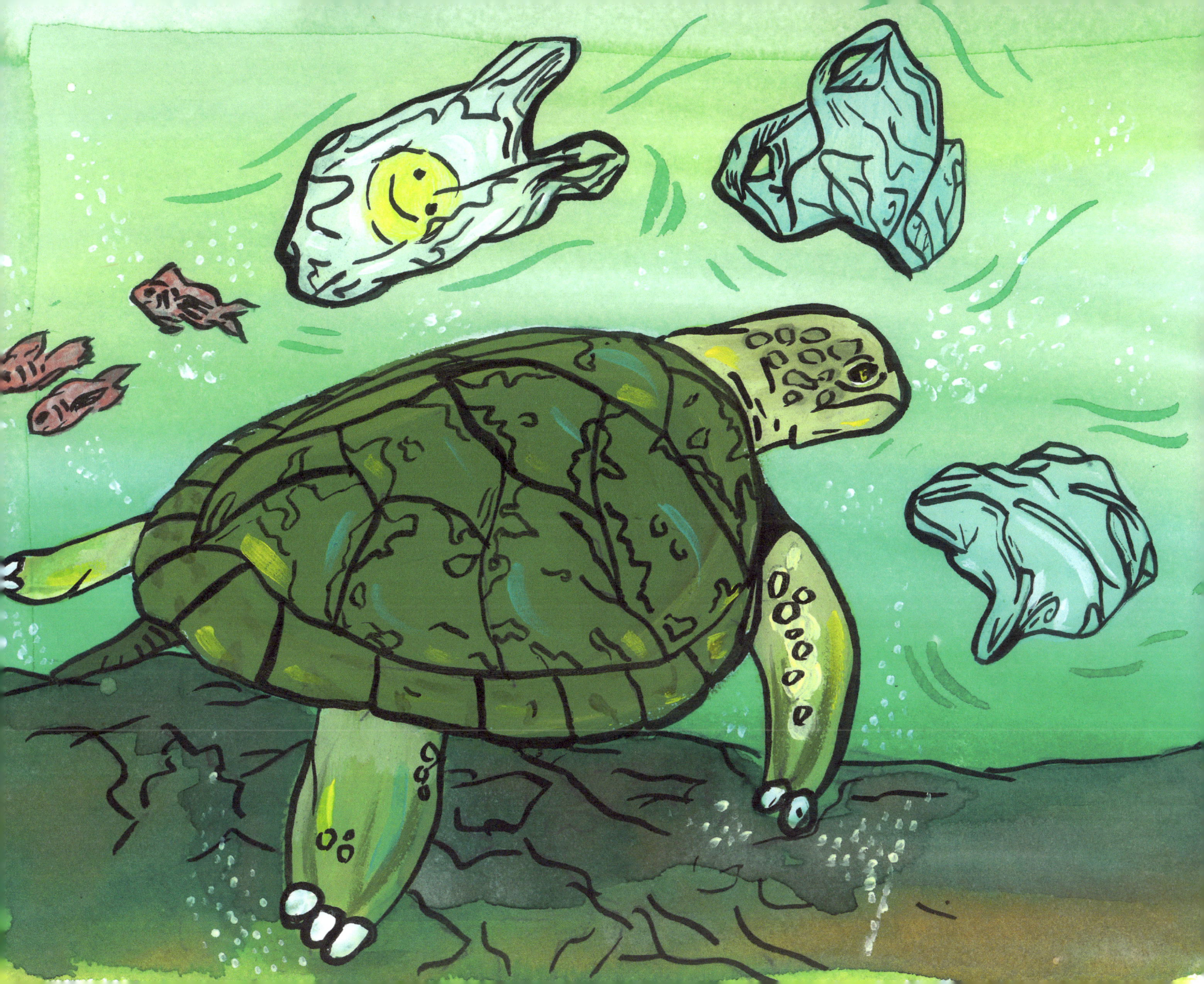

HELP ME... Glub! Glub!

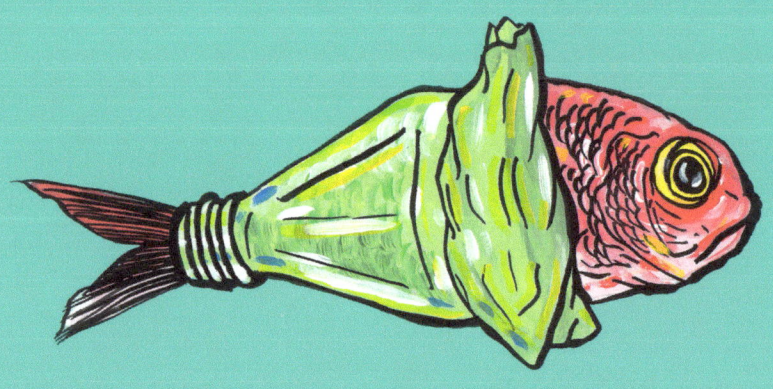

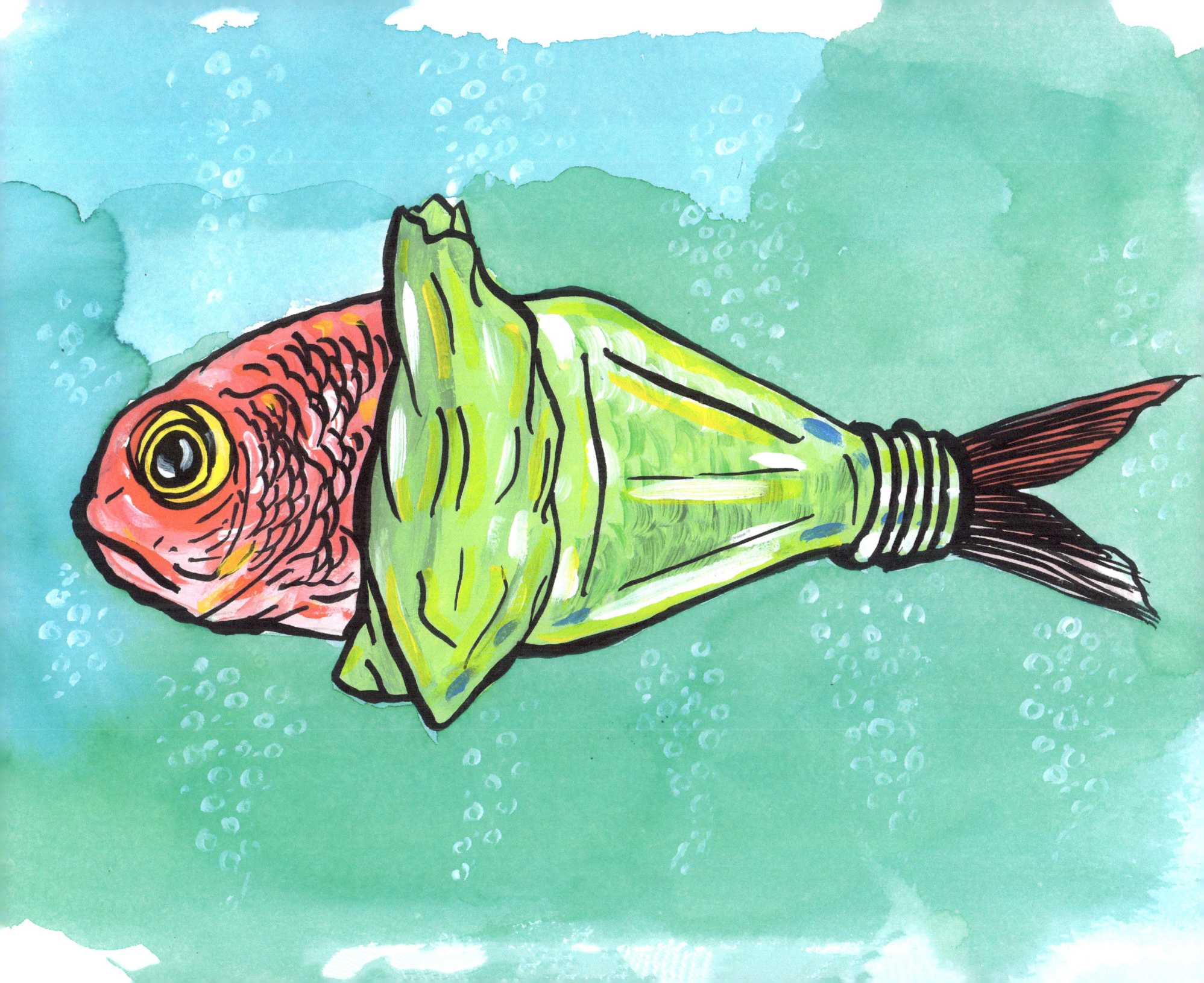

Field 5 at Robert Moses State Park is a favorite. The **w i d e** sandy beach

is always clean, you can build the best sand castles with family and friends.

There is a lovely boardwalk and a snack bar for treats.

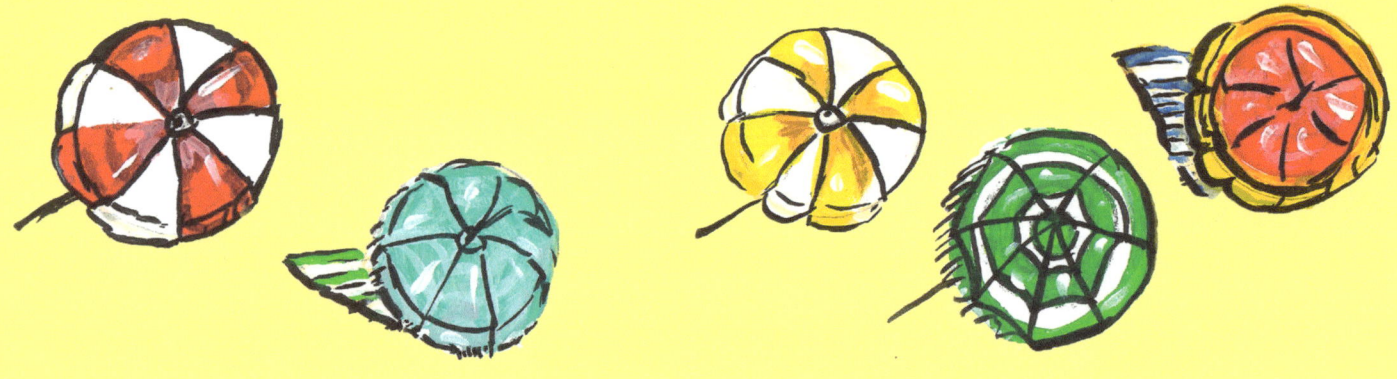

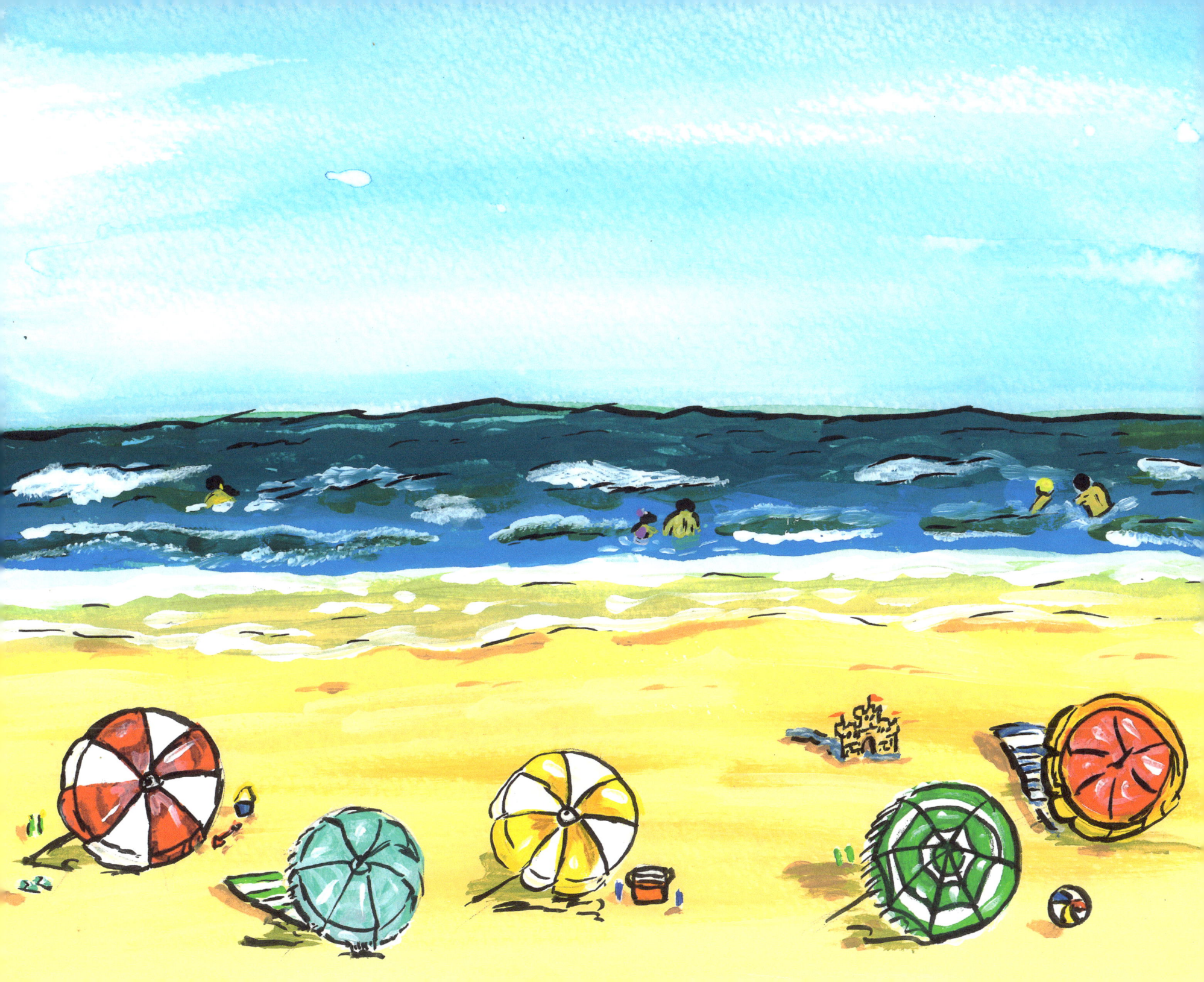

Kids board, fish board, fun board, long board and paddle board. We have some pretty great breaks and some of the most legendary surf shops around.

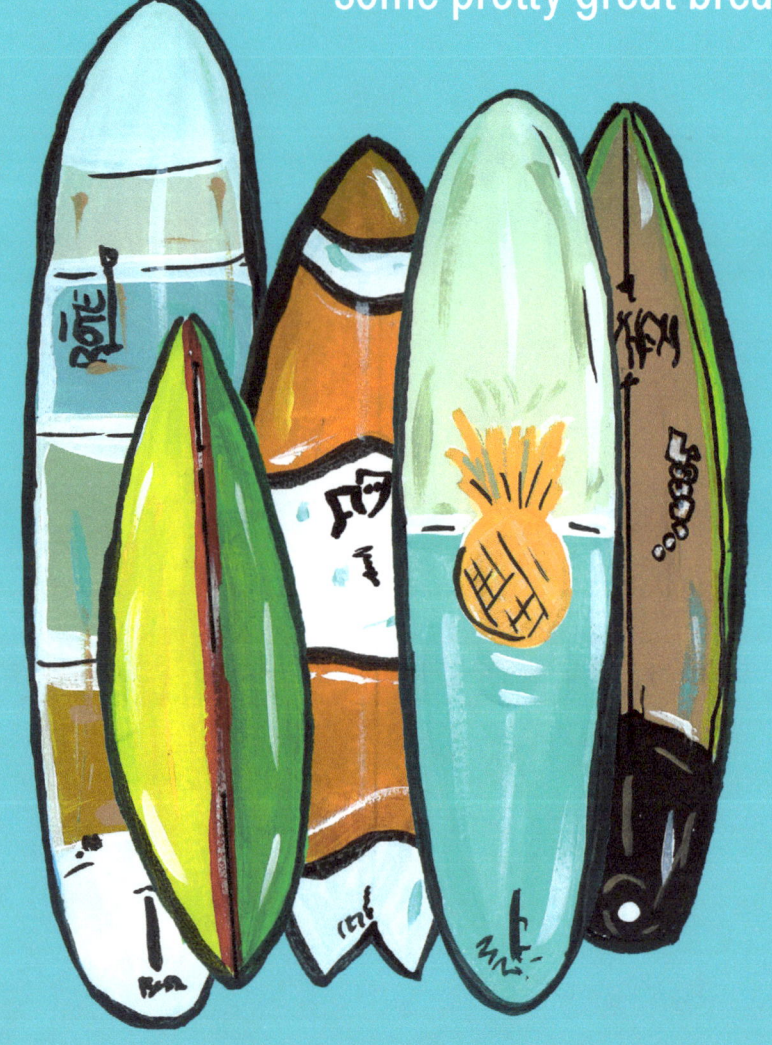

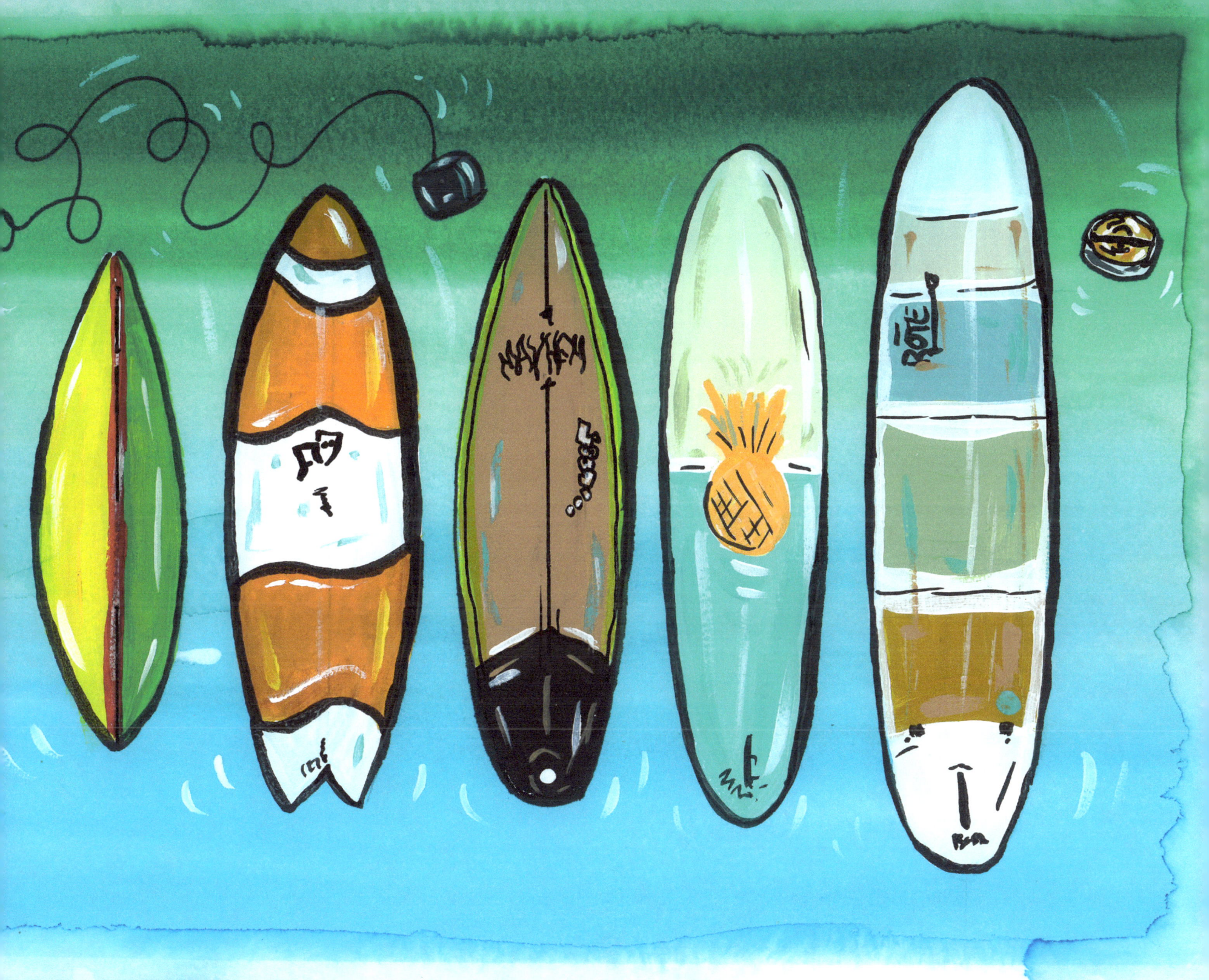

Nothing is more classic on the South Shore of Long Island than an ice cream truck during the summer. They can be spotted rolling down your street or parked at your favorite beach.

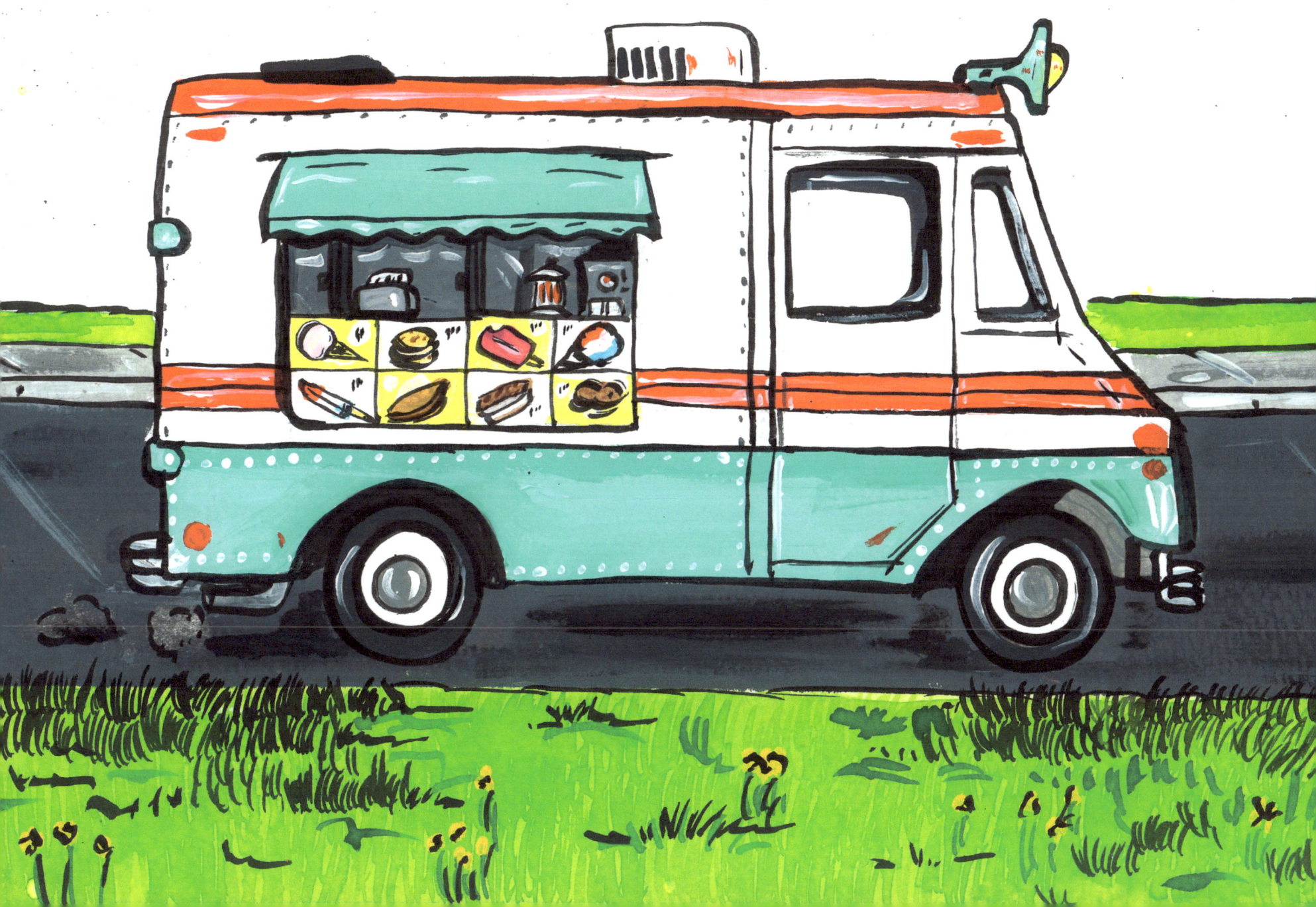

Beach balls, ice cream, swimming, boating, surfing and fishing to just name a few. So many things to enjoy during the hot summer months on The Great South Bay. There is no place I'd rather be any day.

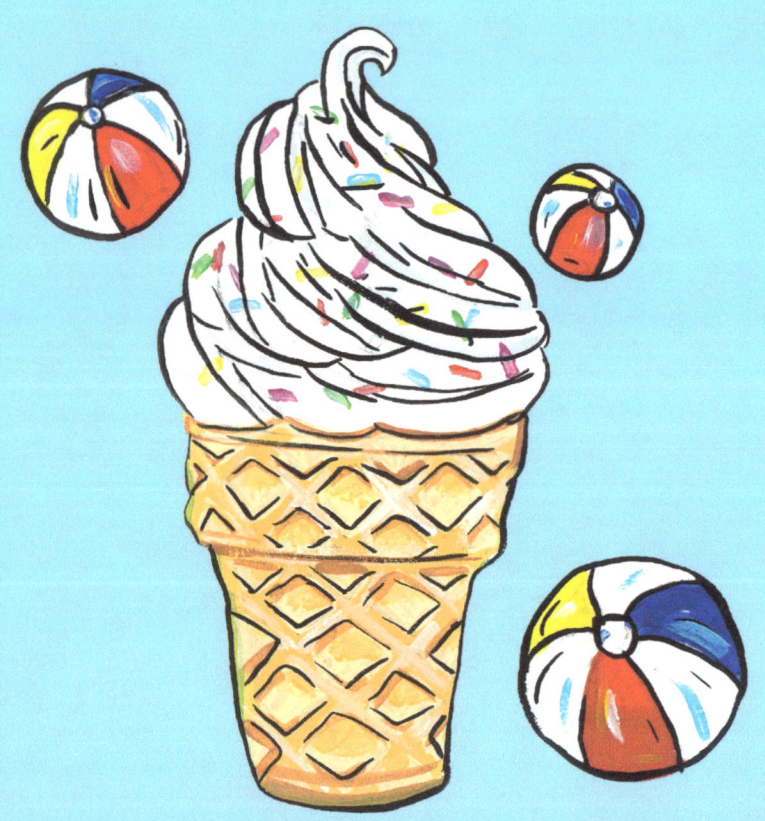

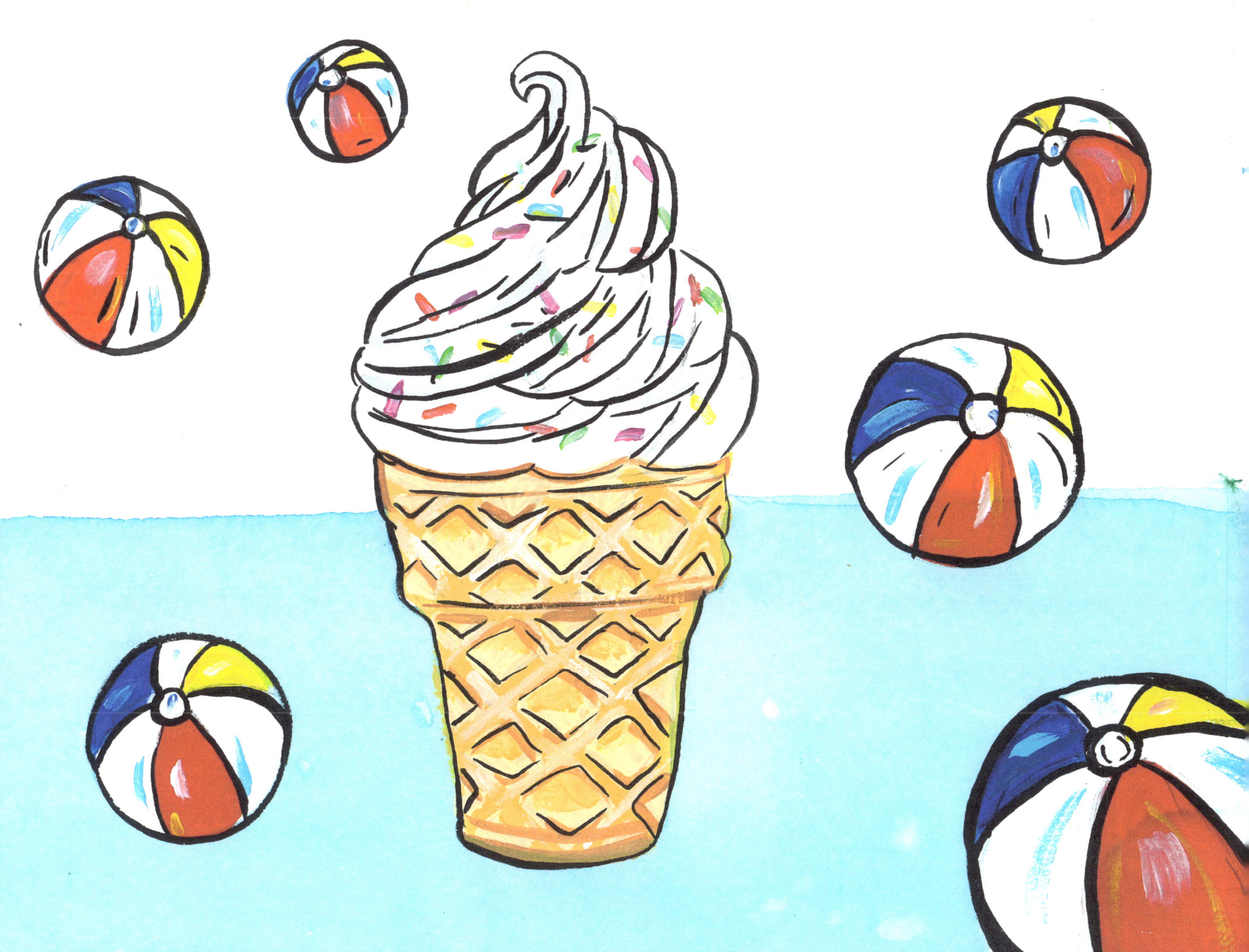